Why the Cross?

Reframing New Testament Theology
Edited by Joel B. Green

Why the Cross?

DONALD SENIOR

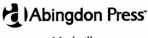

Abingdon Press

Nashville

WHY THE CROSS?
Copyright © 2014 by Abingdon Press

All rights reserved.

This book is printed on acid-free paper.

Library of Congress Cataloging-in-Publication Data

Senior, Donald.
 Why the cross? / Donald Senior.
  pages cm.—(Reframing New Testament theology)
 Includes bibliographical references and index.
 ISBN 978-1-4267-5934-5
 1. Jesus Christ—Crucifixion. I. Title.
 BT453.S395 2014
 232.96´3—dc23

                    2014022530

14 15 16 17 18 19 20 21 22 23—10 9 8 7 6 5 4 3 2 1
MANUFACTURED IN THE UNITED STATES OF AMERICA

Contents

Foreword

At first glance, the phrase "New Testament theology" seems clear enough. However, attempts to explain it immediately expose some speed bumps. Do we want to describe the theology we find in the New Testament? Construct a theology on a New Testament foundation? Or perhaps sketch an account of early Christian beliefs and practices from the New Testament era? This series of books frames the question in a different way: How do we take seriously that, together with the Old Testament, the New Testament has in the past and should in the present inform, form, and transform the church's faith and life?

Almost everyone will agree that the New Testament books concern themselves with *theology*. This truism is supported on almost every page as New Testament writers speak of God, the significance of Jesus of Nazareth for God's agenda for the world, the character of God's people, faithful life before God, and God's coming to set the world right.

How does the New Testament witness relate to the church's life today? This is less clear and therefore more controversial. The church affirms its allegiance to the God of whom scripture speaks and, therefore, ties itself, its faith and witness, to the Old and New Testaments. How the church's affirmations work themselves out in terms of engagement with the New Testament materials—this is the question.

Reframing New Testament Theology gets at this question by encouraging active, theological engagement with the New Testament itself. Readers will find among the books in this series an awareness of the obstacles we face—obstacles like the following:

- New Testament texts were written in another time and another place. In what sense, then, can we say that they were written to us or for us? After all, those first readers of Matthew's Gospel or the Letter of James would be dumbstruck by the idea of streaming video in a church service, just as most of us lack any firsthand experience with anything analogous to the challenges of peasant farmers and fisherfolk in ancient Galilee.

- What of the sheer variety of voices we hear among the New Testament books? If we want the New Testament to help orient our thinking about mission or salvation, how do we make sense of the different perspectives we sometimes encounter? Do we accord privilege to some voices over others? Do we try to synthesize various viewpoints?

- New Testament writers raise issues that may seem foreign to us today and overlook some of our contemporary concerns. Our educational systems, political structures, immigration policies, knowledge of the universe, modes of transportation, and the countless other day-to-day realities that we take for granted separate us from the equally countless assumptions, beliefs, and behaviors that characterized people living in the ancient Mediterranean world. Faced with these differences, how do we work with scripture?

Additionally, our readers will find an awareness of a range of questions about how best to think about "New Testament theology"—questions like these:

- Since the "new" in "New Testament" presumes an "Old Testament," what status should our New Testament theological explorations assign to the Old Testament? How do we understand the theological witness of the New Testament in relation to the Old?

- Are we concerned primarily with what the New Testament writers taught (past tense) their first readers theologically, or do we want to know what the New Testament teaches (present tense) us? Is "New Testament theology" a descriptive task or a prescriptive one?

- Do we learn from the New Testament writers the "stuff" of Christian theology, or do we apprentice ourselves to them so that we might learn how to engage in the theological task ourselves? Does the New

Testament provide the raw material for contemporary theology, or does it invite us into ongoing reflection with it about God and God's ways?

If contributions to this series demonstrate an awareness of obstacles and issues like these, this does not mean that they address them in a uniform manner. Nor are these books concerned primarily with showing how to navigate or resolve conundrums like these. What holds this series together is not a particular set of methodological commitments but a keen sense that scripture has in the past and should in the present instruct and shape the church's faith and life. What does it mean to engage the New Testament from within the church and for the church?

One further consideration: The church turns to the scriptures believing that the Bible is authoritative for what we believe and what we do, but it does so while recognizing that the church's theology is shaped in other ways, too—by God's self-disclosure in God's "book of nature," for example—and in relation to the ecumenical creeds with which the church has identified itself: the Apostles' Creed, the Nicene Creed, and the Athanasian Creed. Not surprisingly, New Testament "theology" invites reflecting on, interacting with, learning from, and sometimes struggling with the scriptures, and doing so in relation to human understanding more generally as well as in the context of our common Christian confessions.

Intended for people interested in the studying the New Testament and the nature of the Christian message and the Christian life, for classrooms, group interaction, and personal study, these volumes invite readers into a conversation with New Testament theology.

Joel B. Green
General Editor

Abbreviations

Introduction

Why the Cross?

The cross is the defining image of Christianity. The cross by itself, or as a *crucifix* with a depiction of the body of Christ fastened to it, is found in countless places: mounted on church steeples, embroidered on sacred vestments, attached to the walls of homes and institutions, tattooed on the hands of Coptic monks, fashioned into jewelry worn by believers as a symbol of their faith and by others as merely as an exotic necklace or earring.

Art historians debate how soon the cross became a widespread symbol in early Christianity. Some believe that this did not occur until well into the fourth century when the more secure place of Christianity in the Constantinian era blunted the "scandal" of promoting a Crucified Christ. However, more recent research has challenged this view. There is compelling evidence that the early Christians used a combined abbreviation of the Greek letters *tau* ("t") and *rho* ("r") found in *stauros*, the Greek word for "cross," as a visual depiction of a crucifix. Such visual abbreviations or *staurograms* are found in some of the earliest manuscript fragments, such as the Bodmer papyrus dating from around 200 CE where quotations from John's Passion Narrative use these staurograms when the word for "cross" appears.[1]

---

1. These staurograms are not abbreviations of key titles or words such as the common Chi Rho, which is an abbreviation of the word "Christ," but a visual representation that depicts the cross ("+") with the outline of a head mounted on it by means of the top of the Greek letter "r," which is similar in appearance to the English alphabet letter "p." See Hurtado, "The Staurogram," 49–52, 63. See also Hurtado, *The Earliest Christian Artifacts*, 135–54. Another example of a possible early depiction of the cross, but one with a very different spirit, is the famous Alexamenos graffiti, which depicts a man (Alexamenos) apparently worshipping a crucified figure who has the head of a donkey. Beneath the figure are the crudely

In any case, we know from the witness of the New Testament writings themselves and later patristic texts that the cross of Christ stood at the center of Christian proclamation. The fact that crucifixion was a feared and heinous form of public execution in the Roman era was a serious complication for a new faith that proclaimed a crucified Jew was in fact the Son of God and for his followers their hope of salvation. But the cross of Christ was too essential to the Christian message to mute reference to it. When Christianity was becoming more well established in the Roman Empire, from the fourth century on, the cross began to appear everywhere as a sign of Christian faith. Byzantine churches would ultimately take on a cruciform design. In Byzantine art, such as frescos, mosaics, and icons, the cross is an ever-present symbol. The characteristic and universal Christian symbol of the cross has remained a consistent trademark throughout the centuries into our own day.[2]

As I will illustrate in the pages that follow, within the New Testament itself and in subsequent Christian theology, the cross takes on a wide range of symbolic meaning. Reflecting the terrible historical reality of crucifixion as a cruel instrument of capital punishment, the cross becomes synonymous with various forms of human suffering. At the same time, as in the theology of John's Gospel, the cross paradoxically becomes the supreme expression of Jesus' giving of his life out of love for his friends. Because Christians view the cross as the definitive means of redemption and atonement from sin, the cross is also viewed as a sign of blessing. Ministers and priests trace the sign of the cross over their congregations as a blessing; Catholic and Orthodox Christians bless themselves with the sign of the cross several times daily. Linked to a belief that through the cross Christ overcame death and evil, the cross is used as an emblem of protection—affixed to church banners, mounted on the walls of homes, lifted on a pole to lead processions and pilgrimages praying for God's protection. In a similar vein, the cross has often been associated with military victory, as in the famous story of Constantine's vision before the Battle of Milvian Bridge and in subsequent centuries where the sign of the cross was painted on the body armor of the Crusaders, mounted on the tombstones of fallen soldiers, and stamped on famous military insignia such as the Victoria Cross.[3]

---

written words: "Alexamenos worships [his] God." Found carved in plaster on a wall on the Palatine hill in Rome, it has been dated without certainty somewhere between the first and third centuries and probably was meant to ridicule Christian belief and practice. See further, Balch and Osiek, *Early Christian Families in Context*, 103–4.

2. See the study of Irvine, *The Cross and Creation in Christian Liturgy and Art*, who traces the central role of the cross in art and liturgy and architecture.

3. On the appropriation of the cross as a military symbol, see the essay of Moltmann, "The Cross as Military Symbol for Sacrifice," in Trelstad, *Cross Examinations*, 259–63.

The Scandal of the Cross

But the cross, both as a sign of human suffering and as a positive sign of blessing and redemption, raises searing questions for Christian belief. Answering the question "Why the cross?" means not only explaining the historical context that led to the crucifixion of Jesus of Nazareth but also understanding how the cross in Christian tradition symbolizes various forms of human suffering past and present. Therefore, the question "Why the cross?" also asks how the reality of human suffering, particularly innocent suffering, fits with Christian belief in a God of love, compassion, and justice. These are serious and difficult questions and, in fact, some traditional Christian answers to these questions themselves become part of the problem.

One might note two fundamental meanings given to the cross based on two characteristic Christian expressions. One is the call to "bear the cross" and the other is "to take up the cross and follow me." Like Simon of Cyrene in the gospel passion accounts, we can be asked to bear a cross we did not choose: a serious illness, the loss of a loved one, failure of a marriage, loss of a job. These sufferings come without invitation and often without warning. And yet traditional Christian wisdom affirms that we are asked "to bear the cross"; to suffer in the spirit of Christ without bitterness or complaint, and, in so doing, we are purified. By contrast, the gospel saying "to take up the cross" implies an intentional and active commitment to follow Christ, including embracing the possibility of rejection and suffering, and even death itself, for the sake of the gospel. Thus "taking up the cross" becomes a way of expressing Christian discipleship and mission undertaken in a deliberate and challenging manner.

One of the most difficult questions the cross of Jesus raises is the issue of innocent suffering. By all accounts Jesus of Nazareth was a "just" man, innocent of the crimes with which he was charged. Yet his innocence did not protect him from terrible suffering—an unjust arrest, interrogation and torture, and death by crucifixion. The fundamental Christian conviction that Jesus was not only innocent but was, in fact, the Son of God, the most noble and sacred human being ever conceived, one whose life was without sin, who embodied the very being of God—this profound faith only makes the question of why Jesus had to suffer more acute. Jesus' final words from the cross, the opening verse of Psalm 22 quoted in both the Gospels of Matthew and Mark, seem to make this very point: "My God, my God, why have you left me?" (Matt 27:46; Mark 15:34).

It is a lament expressed on the lips of parents and spouses and siblings learning of the death of loved one. It is the question that rises in the throats of anyone who has witnessed the horror of a crime scene or viewed the devastation of a suicide bombing or stood at the bedside of a desperately ill child. It is the devastating question raised by the genocide of six million Jews in World War II. How do we reconcile belief in a loving God with the reality of human suffering, particularly innocent suffering? This is a question that the biblical peoples themselves struggled with, from the anguish of Job to the Wisdom of Solomon's wrestling with the suffering of the just man.

Most fundamental of all, Christian faith affirms that the cross of Christ, linked essentially with his resurrection, is a source of redemption and new life. Through the cross of Christ sin is forgiven and the world is reconciled to God—these are deep convictions of the New Testament and consequently of orthodox Christian faith. But here, too, the cross remains an enigma. How exactly does the death of Jesus free us from sin and secure our redemption? What exactly is "saving" about such a hideous form of human suffering and ignominious death? What difference did the death of Jesus on the cross really make? If, as Christian faith also affirms, Jesus Christ is the Word of God incarnate, and if his becoming human revealed God's love for the world and gave humanity a new dignity and even a divine character, why was it necessary for Jesus to also have to suffer and die in order to effect our salvation?

The use of the cross as a symbol for Christian experience and discipleship raises another set of questions, one posed in particular by feminist and womanist theologians.[4] Does the notion of "bearing the cross" imply a kind of passive and subservient acceptance of suffering, particularly of suffering imposed by oppressive and unjust structures and systems? Do such traditional exhortations to "bear the cross," particularly when stated by a patriarchal authority structure in relationship to women's aspirations, make the cross a blunt instrument to keep women "in their place" and to encourage submission and conformity? Have some aspects of traditional piety built around the bearing of the cross and the sufferings of the cross been used to encourage African Americans and other oppressed groups to accept their fate and not redress their rights? Furthermore, does the focus on the silent and uncomplaining bearing the cross of suffering often recommended to persons with disabilities and persons with various forms of illness become a code word that encourages passivity and discourages courageous action demanding access and justice?[5]

In general, does the focus on the cross give Christianity a fundamentally morbid and negative aura? Is not Christian faith rather a celebration of abun-

---

4. See in particular the set of essays in Trelstad, *Cross Examinations*; see also Reid, *Taking Up the Cross*.

5. See Eiesland, *The Disabled God*.

dant life? Does not piety and devotion focused on the passion of Jesus and his death on the cross rob Christianity of its fundamental vibrancy and proclaim not a God of life and love but a God who exacts death to atone for human sinfulness? Does not the focus of traditional Christian theology on the redemptive death of Jesus isolate the meaning of the cross from the overall mission of Jesus as presented in the Gospels, a mission whose keynote was the advent of God's kingdom where suffering and death would be replaced by healing and abundant life? Is not then the theology of the cross ultimately a distortion of the good news proclaimed by Christ?

Why the Cross?

These are serious questions that reach to the heart of Christian faith. And they are all the more serious because they are being raised not by persons hostile to Christianity but by sincere believers who are grappling with the meaning of the cross as a fundamental reality of Christian faith. The study we are about to embark on does not pretend to adequately answer all of these gripping questions. Many of these questions demand an ongoing strong theological and ethical reflection on the part of the church, and the answers may vary from culture to culture and from age to age.

But what this study can do, as this series intends, is to examine in some detail the role and meaning of the cross in the writings of the New Testament. It is here, in this biblical witness, that the church's subsequent theological reflection and the practices of its piety must find their root. To give our task proper focus, we will take our cue primarily from those passages in the New Testament where the cross or crucifixion is explicitly mentioned. In a few instances, there are alternate metaphorical words used for *cross* such as the *tree* or the *wood*, and we will include those texts as well. Understanding the meaning of the cross also means considering the passion stories in the four gospels, for here is where the reality of the cross of Jesus is fully proclaimed, and, to do the Passion Narratives justice, we also have to note their connection to the body of the gospel accounts as a whole. The Passion Narratives in all four gospels do not appear on the scene suddenly and unexpectedly but flow organically from the account of Jesus' public ministry presented in a distinctive and characteristic way in each of the Gospels. When turning to Paul's Letters we will also take our cue from the several highly significant passages where he refers to the cross of Christ, but we will also have to range out into the other aspects of Paul's theology to provide the essential context for his theology of the cross. The same will be true of the other New Testament texts we examine, such as the deuteropauline writings: Colossians, Ephesians, and Hebrews, as well as the First Letter of Peter and Revelation.

Simply noting the various texts that need to be reviewed reminds us at the outset that there is no single or uniform New Testament perspective on the meaning of the cross but a rich diversity of perspective and tone. At the same time, every facet of the New Testament reflections on the meaning of the cross takes its starting point and finds its anchor in the fact that Jesus of Nazareth, Son of God and Messiah, incarnate Word and Savior of the world, died on a cross. No serious student of history, whatever one's estimation of the New Testament or the figure of Jesus himself, could doubt that Jesus of Nazareth was crucified. The approach we are taking, therefore, is first to describe the historical reality of crucifixion as a common form of execution in the ancient world and a form of capital punishment within the Roman Empire. We will then turn to a series of motifs that express the meaning of the cross as reflected in various New Testament texts. We will group these motifs under major headings: (1) The Cross and the Meaning of Human Suffering; (2) The Cross and Salvation; (3) The Cross and Discipleship.

By helping the reader encounter the beauty and power of the New Testament's reflection on the cross, I hope that the meaning of this profound Christian symbol will become clearer and a more satisfying answer can be given to the question, "Why the cross?"

As I complete my work on this volume, some special thanks are in order. First and foremost, I owe gratitude to Joel Green, the general editor of this series and the one who graciously invited me to address this topic. His vision for the series and his guidance and support in helping me along the way were unfailing. Thanks, too, to Kathy Armistead of Abingdon Press for her generous editorial work. I have had the privilege of working with Abingdon Press on several projects and without fail it has been a most satisfying experience. Closer to home, I want to thank Lissa Rommel for her expert help in preparing the manuscript and Catholic Theological Union for giving me a semester's sabbatical that enabled me to complete the project on time.

Finally, I want to dedicate this work to the memory of Frans Neirynck, professor of New Testament at the University of Louvain (1927–2012). Professor Neirynck was my "Doctor Pater," and I realize especially now that his incredible erudition and unyielding dedication to biblical exegesis were a great gift to me in my formative years as a doctoral student. He inspired awe, including raw fear, in his students and faculty colleagues alike, but his generous attention to the work of his doctoral students and his determination that they be successful were remarkable. Under his guidance I first began to explore the passion of Jesus and that subject has been a constant topic of interest ever since.

Chapter One

The Cross and Crucifixion in the First-Century Greco-Roman and Jewish World

The historical background of crucifixion as an extreme and horrifying form of capital punishment provides an essential context for understanding the meaning of the cross in the New Testament.[1] Before the cross took on the powerful symbolic meaning it has for Christian faith, it was already a historical reality known and dreaded by the ancient Mediterranean world.

The origin of crucifixion as a form of capital punishment for criminals or extreme retribution toward an enemy may be traced back to the Persians. The fifth-century BCE historian Herodotus reported that Darius, the emperor of Persia, crucified three thousand inhabitants of Babylon. But references to

---

1. On the historical context of crucifixion, see Hengel, *Crucifixion in the Ancient World and the Folly of the Message of the Cross*; see also Chapman, *Ancient Jewish and Christian Perceptions of Crucifixion*; Cook, "Crucifixion and Burial"; Fitzmyer, "Crucifixion in Ancient Palestine, Qumran Literature, and the New Testament," 493–510; Samuelsson, *Crucifixion in Antiquity*; and Cook, *Crucifixion in the Mediterranean World*.

various forms of crucifixion are found early on in various sectors of the ancient world, and its precise origin is impossible to determine. The Romans may have become aware of crucifixion from their long interaction with Carthage, where this form of punishment was also used. As we will note, it became a more formal mode of capital punishment under Roman law. Crucifixion took a variety of forms, from a crude impaling of a victim on a wooden plank or platform to the more ritualized public act of crucifixion described in the Gospels. In some instances the victims were already dead and their bodies were publicly displayed as a further humiliation or degradation. At other times, crucifixion was the means of death itself, an exceptionally cruel, often slow, and always agonizingly painful process.

Under Roman practice, crucifixion was reserved almost exclusively for noncitizens, particularly slaves and members of the lower classes. In a famous quotation, Cicero in 63 BCE defended his client Rabirius, a Roman senator accused of a grievous crime and threatened with crucifixion, by stating that a Roman citizen, however guilty, should never be subject to such a punishment:

> How grievous a thing it is to be disgraced by a public court; how grievous to suffer a fine, how grievous to suffer banishment; and yet in the midst of any such disaster we retain some degree of liberty. Even if we are threatened with death, we may die free men. But the executioner, the veiling of the head and the very word "cross" should be far removed not only from the person of a Roman citizen but his thoughts, his eyes and his ears. For it is not only the actual occurrence of these things, but the very mention of them, that is unworthy of a Roman citizen and a free man.[2]

As suggested in Cicero's rhetoric, while crucifixion was not infrequent in the Roman world, there are relatively few references to it in ancient texts and even less detailed descriptions of it because it was an odious subject not to be dwelt on. Even the restrained descriptions of Jesus' crucifixion in the gospel accounts are more detailed than most ancient references to this practice. Crucifixion was known according to Cicero as the *summum supplicium* (the "ultimate punishment") or in the Roman historian Tacitus's famous phrase, the *mors turpissima crucis* ("the most terrible death of the cross"), and by the first century Jewish historian Josephus as "the most pitiable of human deaths," ranked first above burning and beheading in the hierarchy of terrible forms of punishment.[3]

While the process of crucifixion took various forms, the general features

---

2. Cicero, *Pro Rabirio Perduellionis Reo*, 16.

3. Josephus, *Wars of the Jews*, 7:203.

are consistent. In many cases the victim, whether a condemned criminal or a captive, was first tortured, often in the form of flogging, as in the case of Jesus in the gospel accounts. Seneca, for example, makes the case that it is better to commit suicide than to submit to death by crucifixion and, in describing the agony of such a death, refers to "ugly welts" on the shoulders and chest of the victims—wounds most likely inflicted by flogging.[4] In some instances, the severity of such torture had the effect of hastening death—as may be the case with the crucifixion of Jesus. Crosses themselves had different shapes, either a single stake to which the victim was fastened or equipped with a cross beam as in the classical depiction of the cross. Depending on circumstances, the condemned person was made to carry the crossbeam to the site of the execution.

The place of execution was normally in public view. Roman rhetorician Quintilian (35–95 CE) emphasized the deterrent effect of having crucifixions in public places: "Whenever we crucify the guilty, the most crowded roads are chosen, where the most people can see and be moved by this fear. For penalties relate not so much to retribution as to their exemplary effect."[5] One of the major rationales for crucifixion was to discredit the cause and example of the one crucified. This is why it was applied especially to crimes of treason, sedition, robbery, and other actions that disturbed the public order—particularly on the part of slaves. On the way to execution, condemned criminals might also carry a sign or *titulus* that indicated the nature of their crime; in some instances—as in the case of Jesus—the titulus would be fastened to the cross to inform the public about the nature of the condemned person's crime.

Once at the execution site, the victims were fastened to the cross, either by tying them with ropes or, as was often the case, by nailing their hands and feet to the beam. To keep the body from sagging too much, the victim was often supported by a wooden peg or small seat. A rare find of the remains of a crucified man buried near Jerusalem at Giv'at ha-Mivtar demonstrated that at least the feet of this victim were nailed to the cross.[6] Death could come slowly, with the victim eventually expiring through a combination of asphyxiation, dehydration, or brutal trauma caused by attacks of animals or birds while the victim was pinned helpless to the cross. Exposed in a public setting, the

---

4. Seneca, Epistle 101 to Lucilius.

5. Quintilian, *The Lesser Declamations. N. 274.*

6. At first archaeologists examining the remains concluded that the man's feet were fastened to the cross by a single nail driven through his ankles. Further examination suggests that each of his feet were nailed separately to the upright stake of the cross and that his hands and torso were tied to the cross by ropes. The fact remains that this find confirms the basic method of crucifixion and that the victim was later allowed to be buried in a family tomb. See further, Zias and Sekeles, "The Crucified Man from Giv'at ha-Mivtar."

victims would also be the object of taunts and derision from passing crowds, as also reflected in the gospel accounts. Josephus reports that during the siege of Jerusalem, the Romans, in public view of the city, crucified large numbers of Jews who were trying to escape the siege, pinning their bodies to crosses in grotesque postures to add to their ridicule and also to put fear into the Jews who were defending the walls.[7]

As part of the intended humiliation and dishonoring of the victims, corpses could be left on the cross for days after the death of the crucified, with their bodies exposed to visible decomposition and the attacks of animals and birds. Roman records indicate that the remains of those crucified would ultimately be thrown into public common graves set aside for this purpose. But there is also evidence, as in the case of the gospel accounts of Joseph of Arimathea, who sought permission from Pilate to have the body of Jesus buried, that relatives or friends could request permission to bury victims of crucifixion, even if they were notorious criminals or rebels. Permission for this was usually given, although in certain cases, depending on the notoriety of the victim and the whims of the authorities, it could be refused.[8]

As noted, this terrible form of death was rarely inflicted on Roman citizens but was reserved for all practical purposes for slaves, members of the lower classes, and foreigners. While robbers and bandits were fair game for this punishment because they were a threat and disturbed the good order of the Roman world, crucifixion of slaves was not uncommon. Roman society had a great fear of slave revolt, and slaves who joined in any form of sedition or who appeared in any way to plot against their masters were subject to crucifixion. The famous morbid prediction of the slave Sceledrus about his own fate reflects this: "I know the cross will be my grave: that is where my ancestors are, my father, grandfathers, great-grandfathers, great-great-grandfathers."[9] Horace refers to a notorious example of a slave threatened with crucifixion because he dared to sample his master's fish soup while bringing it to the table.[10] Under Nero, slaves who were members of a household in which the master had been murdered could also be crucified as a deterrent for any who might have been accessory to such a crime. Likewise, even to consult an astrologer about the fate of one's master could make one liable to this capital punishment.

While crucifixion was frequently used as the supreme capital punishment

---

7. Josephus, *Wars of the Jews*, 5.449–51 and 2.75.

8. See Cook, "Crucifixion and Burial."

9. Titus Maccius Plautus, *The Miles gloriosus of Titus Maccius Plautus*, 372–73 (ca. 205 BCE).

10. Horace, *Satires*, 1.3.80.

in the Roman Empire, the infliction of this torment on Jews by Jews was far more rare. Josephus reports that under the Hasmonean dynasty, the high priest Alexander Janneus (103–76 BCE) had eight hundred Pharisees crucified and the members of their families executed as well. Such atrocities, it should be noted, came during a time when Greco-Roman influence was making inroads into Jewish life. Josephus reports that under the Seleucid dynasty of Antiochus IV in the third century BCE numerous Jews were crucified for resistance based on fidelity to the Jewish law.[11] One important religious note specific to the Jewish context that we will turn to later is the tradition founded on Deuteronomy 21:22-25 in a section dealing with violent crime: "If someone is guilty of a capital crime, and they are executed, and you then hang them on a tree, you must not leave the body hanging on the tree but must bury it the same day because God's curse is on those who are hanged. Furthermore, you must not pollute the ground that the LORD your God is giving to you as an inheritance." Although its meaning is somewhat obscure, this text probably refers to the public display of a body of someone who suffered capital punishment by some other means and then hung in public display. This display is tempered by the injunction that the body must be buried by sundown. The fact that such a fate is seen as a sign that the condemned person is also cursed by God adds to the sense of horror and perhaps acted as a constraint on any Jewish adaptation of this form of capital punishment. In texts from Qumran, the curse of Deuteronomy 21:22-23 was applied to those who were crucified.[12] Paul will refer to the Deuteronomy text in Galatians 3:13 in connection with the crucifixion of Jesus.[13] On the other hand, during Roman governance of Judea and Samaria and later of the entire region, crucifixion of Jews by Romans was well known. This was particularly true during the periods of the Jewish revolt (66–73 CE; 132 CE); crimes of sedition by slaves, noncitizens, and "foreigners" were considered particularly heinous and deserving of the supreme punishment from the Roman point of view.

This brief review of the historical practice of crucifixion, particularly under the Roman imperium, reveals certain constant traits:

1. Crucifixion was primarily a military and political punishment, used as triumphant retribution and an instrument of fear for defeated enemy combatants or as a deterrent for those who would dare to attempt treason or acts of sedition against civil authority. A particular

---

11. Josephus, *Wars of the Jews*, 1.97–98.

12. Pesher Nahum.

13. See below, p. 90.

5

fear in this instance was the possibility of violence or uprisings on the part of slaves. Robbery, banditry, and other forms of serious disturbance of the public order also fell under the threat of crucifixion, because they were seen ultimately as a threat to civil authority.

2. Crucifixion had a public character, carried out near busy thoroughfares or in full view of the enemy. The drawn-out character of this form of execution, with either the victim dying a slow death or the displaying of an already dead corpse for several days, compounded the intended humiliation and discrediting of the victim. Thus crucifixion was intended not only to punish the perpetrator but also to thoroughly discredit and delegitimize the cause for which the perpetrator stood and to reaffirm the political and military might of the one authorizing the crucifixion.

3. Crucifixion was reserved almost exclusively for slaves and lower classes or aliens who had no claim to civic rights. Roman citizens were usually exempt and, if they were also members of the elite, crucifixion was not to be applied even if their crime was judged deserving of death.

4. Although limited to negative connotations, the cross did take on some nonreligious metaphorical meaning in Greco-Roman culture. Gallows humor on the part of slaves saw their fate as death on the cross.[14] A more pertinent example is the romanticized story of M. Atilius Regulus, a Roman general captured by the Carthaginians and sent back to Rome to negotiate peace with Rome. Instead of carrying out the Carthaginians' instructions, Regulus urged the Roman Senate to stiffen their resistance to Carthage. Because he had taken an oath to return to Carthage after his mission, Regulus did so and the furious Carthaginians executed him by crucifixion. This heroic deed was celebrated in later Roman tradition, including the works of Cicero. The second-century CE writer Silius Italicus speaks poetically of Regulus "being hung high upon the tree and (seeing) Italy from his lofty cross."[15] Even more pertinent is the metaphorical use of the cross in some Latin literature as an extreme form of suffering now applied to the pain caused by "desire" or other forms of psychological

---

14. See the quote of Sceledrus cited earlier, p. 14.

15. Quoted in Hengel, *Crucifixion*, 65. See in particular Hengel's treatment of the metaphorical and philosophical use of the terms "cross" or "crucifixion"; 64–68.

suffering or difficulties, such as the legal attacks of an opponent or the suffering of those who have yielded to the unbridled desires of their bodies. Hengel speculates that much of this type of metaphorical use was triggered "by Plato's remark in the *Phaedo* (83cd) that every soul is fastened to the body by desire as though by a nail."[16] It is noteworthy that all of these metaphorical uses of the cross are in negative contexts, speaking of various forms of human suffering.

From this brief review of the historical context of *cross* and *crucifixion* in the ancient Greco-Roman and Jewish contexts, we can already note some connections to the Christian use of these same terms in the New Testament. Ultimately the answer to the question "Why the cross?" must take into account both its historical reality and the range of its symbolic meaning. The connections noted here will be taken up in more detail in the pages that follow:

1. The terrible form of human suffering involved in crucifixion and the revulsion with which first-century peoples viewed this form of capital punishment help explain why Paul, for example, would refer to the "scandal" or "offense" of the cross (1 Cor 1:23; Gal 5:11). The bold Christian message that proclaimed that a Jew who was crucified by the Romans was in fact the Son of God and the awaited deliverer of Israel could only be viewed as "foolishness" to Gentiles and a "scandal" to Jews (1 Cor 1:23). Paul is expressing what must have been the initial reaction to the Christian message on the part of many first-century listeners.

2. The fact that crucifixion was a punishment reserved primarily for slaves, lower classes, and foreigners without rights—what the majority might view as the dregs of society—brings a startling depth of meaning to the association of Jesus with the poor and the outcasts in the gospel literature and underscores the radical nature of the incarnation. Paul's assertions that Christ became sin for us (2 Cor 5:21) and "[became] a curse for us" (Gal 3:13) are surely connected with the ultimate degradation implied in the fate of one who was crucified. So, too, is the phrase that may have been added by Paul to the early Christian hymn in Philippians that expresses the ultimate humiliation

16. Ibid., 67.

7

of the Christ who put aside his equality with God to become a "slave" and to experience, as a slave would, "death on the cross" (Phil 2:7-8). The fact that Jesus was crucified by Roman authority in Jerusalem in the early decades of the first century also affirms in a radical way the reality of the incarnation. Jesus lived and died in a particular time and place; his life was not an abstraction but genuine. The person and message of Jesus are grounded in history.[17]

3. An important function of crucifixion as a public and horrendous form of capital punishment was its deterrent power. The slow and ignominious death of the crucified was an emphatic no to the cause or stance of the one so put to death. If an enemy challenged the might of Rome, crucifixion definitively rejected that challenge. If slaves dared to contemplate revolt against their masters, punishment by crucifixion reaffirmed the authority of the master and crushed the illicit aspiration of the slave. If a violent criminal disregarded public order and the authority of the empire that stood behind it, death by crucifixion reestablished both public order and the absolute power of civil authority. Seen in this light, the crucifixion of Jesus by his opponents was intended as a thundering no to him, to his claims of religious authority, and to his vision of the reign of God embodied in the commitments of his entire ministry. The crucifixion of Jesus, in effect, becomes the "no" side of one of the earliest interpretations of the salvific meaning of the death and resurrection of Jesus. Where crucifixion and death place a no on Jesus, through resurrection God transforms that no into a resounding yes!

4. Finally, the entire public character of crucifixion provides a connection to Christian proclamation. Jesus did not die in the privacy of his home or hidden from public view. The whole ritual of crucifixion, from official condemnation and torture through to the impalement on the cross in full view of passing crowds, makes the death of Jesus a public act. The gospel accounts accentuate this by drawing attention to the title fixed to the cross of Jesus: *Jesus the Nazarene, the king of the Jews* (John 19:19). Thus the death of Jesus as a public act was, in effect, the "word of the cross," conveying a message that would be

---

17. On the historical grounding of Jesus, see Schnelle, *Apostle Paul*, 430–32. "Paul holds fast to the cross as the historical location of the love of God. He resists a complete kerygmatizing of the unique historical event. God's time-transcending act identifies itself as salvific because it has a real place and real time, a name and a history" (431).

complemented and transformed by the resurrection but with the cross remaining an essential component for Christian understanding of the person and mission of Jesus and its impact on the world. In the resurrection appearances found in both Luke and John, the risen Christ still bears the wounds of crucifixion (Luke 24:39-40; John 20:20, 24-29). A word of death intended by crucifixion on the part of his opponents is transformed into a word of life by the one who hangs on the cross and whose death gives way to resurrection.

Chapter Two

The Cross and Human Suffering

In its original, historical context crucifixion represented a feared instrument of ultimate retribution and punishment; however, the death of Jesus Christ on a cross forever changed the meaning of crucifixion from the perspective of Christian faith. A symbol that had a basic univocal meaning as a sign of death in its most extreme and degrading form was transformed into a symbol capable of expressing a variety of life-giving meanings for Christians who believe in Jesus as the Christ and Son of God.

I. The Cross and the Humanity of Jesus

One of the most fundamental meanings ascribed to the cross of Jesus was one that remains close to the historical meaning of crucifixion as an extreme form of human suffering. The fact that Jesus of Nazareth endured death on a cross affirms in the starkest terms the reality of the incarnation. The church's formal creedal statement affirming both the authentic humanity and true divinity of Jesus Christ comes, after decades of Christian reflection and debate, with the formulation of the Council of Chalcedon in 451 CE. However, the conviction that Jesus was truly human as well as divine was already strongly affirmed in the New Testament itself.

11

The Testimony of John's Gospel

The beautiful prologue of John's Gospel (1:1-18), which may have originated as an early Christian hymn, affirms in poetic form the humanity of Jesus. The Word (*logos*) that was with God from the beginning and the Word that in fact was *theos*, or God, descends through the layers of the universe, both through creation as a whole and into the "world" of humanity itself, and then at the climax of the descent, the Word becomes "flesh" (1:14).[1] The word John uses in this key verse is not "body" (Greek = *sōma*) but "flesh," the Greek word *sarx*, which clearly affirms the humanity of Jesus in vivid terms. The term *sarx*/flesh connotes human mortality and limitation; "flesh," as contrasted with "spirit" (*pneuma*), is coupled to death. Paul uses the term "flesh" in a similar way, and it was so used in Greco-Roman philosophical texts.[2]

The Word's "becoming flesh" and "dwelling among us" enables the community who articulates the hymn to *see* the "glory" of the Word made flesh. The term *doxa* or "glory" is used in the Septuagint (Greek) version of the Old Testament to translate the Hebrew word *kabod*, which literally means "heaviness" but is used metaphorically in several passages of the Old Testament to describe the "manifest presence" of God among the people.[3] What John's Gospel articulates here is the foundation of the Christian doctrine of the incarnation. The eternal Word who is *theos* or God truly "becomes flesh," that is, becomes human and makes manifest the hidden presence of God through his very humanness.

While the rhetoric of John's Gospel as a whole gives it something of a transcendent character, there is no doubt that John wants to affirm the true humanity of Jesus. Jesus is the one who gives his "flesh" for the life of the world (6:51), and it is that flesh that will suffer the ignominy of torture and crucifixion, including a lance thrust into the side of the dead Jesus—the only reference to the bleeding body of Jesus in the entire gospel literature.[4] Thus "becoming flesh" for John's Gospel does not merely refer to the conception or birth of Jesus but to the entire historical existence of Jesus; in becoming flesh Jesus becomes truly human and therefore also will endure the full spectrum of human experience, which includes opposition, rejection, and ultimately death.

---

1. In describing the descent of the Word, the prologue at first uses imagery drawn from the creation account in Genesis to describe all things (*panta*) that came to be: "life," "light," "darkness" (1:2-5); subsequently the hymn refers to the "cosmos" or "world," which infers the human realm, capable of accepting or rejecting the Word (1:10-13).

2. See Schnelle, *Apostle Paul*, 340–42.

3. See Exod 16:7-10; 24:17. See also R. Brown, *The Gospel according to John I–XII*, appendix 1, pp. 503–4.

4. In Luke 22:44, Luke refers to Jesus' perspiring heavily "as if" with drops of blood.

The Testimony of Paul

The essential link between being human and experiencing suffering can also be found in the famous hymn cited by Paul in his Letter to the Philippians (2:5-11). In a pattern similar to the prologue of John's Gospel, this poetic reflection on the incarnation has a "descent" pattern, probably influenced in part by Jewish reflection on the personification of Wisdom, who begins at the side of God and enters the human realm and dwells among mortals as an expression of God's presence.[5] Paul quotes this hymn in an effort to discourage factionalism among his beloved community in Philippi by encouraging them to consider the humility and ardent love of Christ Jesus himself for them.[6] The hymn moves from the portrayal of Christ as "in the form of God" but then "he emptied himself by taking the form of a slave and by becoming like human beings." The human Christ "humbled himself by becoming obedient to the point of death, even death on a cross" (Phil 2:8). The hymn will conclude with the triumphant "ascent" of Jesus who is exalted by God and is worthy of homage by every creature "in heaven, on earth, and under the earth."

What is noteworthy for our purposes is that the humanness of Christ is anchored by reference to his "death on a cross." Interpreters debate whether this phrase was an original part of the hymn or, more likely, added by Paul to emphasize the reality of Christ's humanness. The death of Jesus on the cross is the anchor of Paul's Christology and the antidote to any false gospel that would proclaim a Christ who was a demigod and not truly a crucified savior.[7] We should note, too, the connection implicit in the hymn between Jesus' status as a "slave" and his "death on the cross." As noted above, slaves were much more likely to experience the dreaded fate of crucifixion compared to any other rank in Roman society. By affirming that Jesus was both a slave and suffered crucifixion, Paul has gone as far as one could to stress the reality of Jesus' humanness. As Hengel noted in his classic study of crucifixion, those who wish to mute the humanity of Jesus have to separate him from his death on the cross.[8]

The Passion Narratives and the Suffering of the Human Jesus

The New Testament affirmation of Jesus' authentic humanness comes not only through the eloquent testimonies found in the Gospel of John and

5. Compare Prov 8:22-31 and Wis 9:9-10; see further, Thurston, *Philippians & Philemon*, 85.

6. See Frederickson, *Eros and the Christ*. Frederickson emphasizes that that this is the whole point of Paul's citation of the hymn.

7. See below, pp. 88–89

8. Hengel, *Crucifixion*, 15–21.

13

Paul's Letters but also massively through the gospel Passion Narratives. Each evangelist portrays the passion of Jesus in a distinctive way that harmonizes with the character of their gospel as a whole; yet all strongly affirm the reality of the incarnation and the profound sharing of Jesus in the experience of human suffering.[9]

The Passion Narratives portray, as if in slow motion, the inexorable immersion of Jesus into suffering and death. In the Synoptic Gospels there are a series of preparatory scenes, noting the plot of the leaders against Jesus, fueled by the betrayal of Judas, one of the Twelve. These scenes of treachery and betrayal are contrasted in Mark and Matthew with the beautiful account of the anointing of Jesus for burial by an anonymous woman in Bethany.[10] There then follows the preparation for and celebration of the Last Passover meal, where Jesus gives a final interpretation of the meaning of his impending death through the symbolic breaking of the bread and the pouring out of the cup. John's account, as is usually the case, is unique. The account of the Passover meal found in the Synoptics gives way to a long farewell discourse of Jesus, beginning with the departure of Judas on his mission of betrayal and the eloquent symbolic action of the foot washing. The Farewell Discourse, which is an exquisite distillation of Johannine theology and its portrayal of the meaning of Jesus' death and exaltation, take up the remaining section of John 13 through 17.

The Synoptic Gospels conclude the preparation for the passion event with the account of Jesus' anguished prayer in Gethsemane (Matt 26:36-46; Mark 14:32-42; Luke 22:39-46). Jesus laments the specter of his impending death and prays both for deliverance from death and for the strength to accept God's will. This scene, which has echoes in John 12:27-33 and Hebrews 5:7-10, is a powerful affirmation of Jesus' humanity. Rather than a stoic indifference toward the threat of suffering or a Platonic, grateful anticipation of release of his immortal soul from his mortal body, the Jesus of the Gospels fears death and prays to be spared from it.[11] At the same time, his profound trust in his Father and his unswerving fidelity to God tempers his anguish.

Beginning with the arrest, all four gospels narrate the series of humilia-

9. On distinctive theologies of the gospel Passion Narratives, see R. Brown, *The Death of the Messiah*; Carroll and Green, *The Death of Jesus in Early Christianity*; Green, *The Death of Jesus*; Matera, *Passion Narratives and Gospel Theologies*; Senior, *The Passion of Jesus in the Gospel of Matthew*; *The Passion of Jesus in the Gospel of Mark*; *The Passion of Jesus in the Gospel of Luke*; *The Passion of Jesus in the Gospel of John*.

10. Luke does not include this scene, perhaps because he has already introduced a similar incident of anointing in 7:35-50. John (12:1-18) identifies the woman as Mary, the sister of Lazarus.

11. On this contrast between the Platonic view of death as liberation from the body and the Semitic perspective reflected in Jesus' prayer for deliverance from death, see the famous essay of Cullmann, "Immortality of the Soul or Resurrection of the Dead?," in Stendahl, *Immortality and Resurrection*, 207–17.

tions and sufferings inflicted on Jesus that lead to his crucifixion. He is first arrested by stealth in the Garden of Gethsemane. A band of police sent by the religious authorities and led by the betrayer Judas now appears.[12] The disciples at first act with bravado, offering to strike out against the arresting band, but in the Synoptic accounts they ultimately lose heart and flee in fear.[13] In John's account, where Jesus' majesty and authority remain close to the surface of the passion story, Jesus deliberately dismisses his disciples and offers himself to the cowering members of the arresting band. There then follows a series of hearings (more likely a kind of an informal judicial meeting rather than a formal trial) before the religious authorities with Jesus roughly interrogated by Caiaphas, the high priest. (In John's account, Jesus is taken first to Annas, the father-in-law of Caiaphas, and only later to Caiaphas himself. See John 18:13-14, 24.)

Judging Jesus as guilty and worthy of death, the authorities take him to the Roman procurator Pilate, who has come up to Jerusalem from Caesarea Maritima, the seat of Roman governance for Judea and Samaria, to help ensure order during the Passover festival, when the city would swell with pilgrims. Pilate interrogates this Jewish prisoner somewhat laconically but ultimately is swayed by the mounting intensity of the leaders' protests and their successful agitation of the crowds that have gathered.

Pilate tries to deflect the crowd's condemnation by offering the release of Barabbas as a gesture during the Passover festival, but his offer is rejected.[14] When Pilate yields to the wishes of the leaders and the crowds, he condemns Jesus to die by crucifixion, first having him scourged and tortured by the soldiers, who crudely mock his supposed aspiration to kingship, which was one of the charges of sedition hurled at Jesus during his trial. As noted earlier, torture, often by flogging of those condemned to crucifixion, is attested in Roman documentation.[15] In John's account alone, Pilate presents the battered figure of Jesus to the crowds as a last failed attempt to win his freedom (see 19:1-7).

---

12. John's Gospel, by referring to a *speiran* ("cohort"), implies that Roman soldiers also accompanied the police sent by the religious leaders (see John 18:3). This would not be historically implausible. While the Romans were the ultimate governing authority over the province of Judea, which had Jerusalem as its capital, they also entrusted maintenance of public order to the Jewish authorities. In a case with a more dangerous potential, Romans could have been involved. This perspective is reflected in the warning of Caiaphas found in John 11:45-53.

13. Luke, however, remains silent about the disciples' flight (see 22:24-62).

14. The custom of releasing a prisoner on the Passover festival is not attested apart from the gospel accounts yet is historically plausible. Matthew heightens the tension of the choice by identifying Barabbas as "Jesus Barabbas" and Jesus as "Jesus who is called Christ" (see Matt 27:17).

15. See earlier, p. 3.

Jesus is then led to the place of crucifixion, which is identified by John as "Golgotha," Hebrew for the "place of the skull" (John 19:17). While not explicitly stated, the setting, as was normally the case for crucifixion sites, seems to be a public byway where witnesses and passersby could view those crucified. But the Gospels do not elaborate on the moment of pinning Jesus' body to the cross—what must have been a moment of excruciating pain for the victims of crucifixion. Mark, for example, notes with an economy of words, "They crucified him. They divided up his clothes, drawing lots for them to determine who would take what" (15:24).[16]

In each of the gospel accounts, death comes relatively swiftly for the Crucified Jesus—again a detail not without plausibility given the weakened condition of Jesus through his earlier interrogation, torture, and especially flogging, which would have caused a significant loss of blood. Mark, followed by Matthew and Luke, indicates that Jesus hung on the cross for approximately six hours, from nine in the morning until three in the afternoon. John's Gospel does not note the starting time but does appear to agree with the Synoptic version by having the death of Jesus confirmed before the onset of the Passover festival (which would have begun at dusk; see John 19:31).

The moment of Jesus' death is described succinctly and in tones reflecting the theological perspectives of each of the Gospels, yet without doubt each of the Gospels testify to the finality of Jesus' death as he "expires" (Mark 15:37 and Luke 23:46), "yields up his spirit" (Matthew 27:50), or "hands over his spirit" (John 19:30).

The burial of Jesus follows in each of the passion accounts and further affirms that Jesus has been struck by death. In all four accounts, Joseph of Arimathea procures from Pilate permission to bury the body of Jesus. As noted earlier, this practice of a family member or friend seeking permission to bury the victim of crucifixion is also attested in historical records beyond the Gospels. Joseph would prepare the body for burial and have it placed in his own family tomb. Later, after the Sabbath, the women disciples of Jesus would come to complete the burial anointing.

The Gospels, therefore, clearly affirm that Jesus of Nazareth, the one whom the early Christians confessed as the Christ, as Lord and Son of God, as unique revealer of God and God's will, as Savior of the world, was also subject to an ignominious death by crucifixion. Whatever insight into the divine identity of Jesus was proclaimed by the faith of the early church, this

---

16. Mark 15:24; similarly Matthew 27:15, Luke 23:34, and John 19:23-24. John, however, notes that they did not divide his seamless cloak but cast lots for it (19:23-24), most likely a symbolic description on the part of John. See the discussion of the various meanings ascribed to this incident in John in R. Brown, *The Death of the Messiah*, 995–98.

could never offset the reality of his humanity, confirmed by the manner of his dying.[17]

II. The Cross of Jesus as Protest against Injustice and Evil in All Its Forms

The Gospels also affirm that the Crucified Jesus is innocent of the charges brought against him. His condemnation and death were unjust. Yet at the same time, the Gospels do not portray Jesus as a passive victim. Jesus was a healer and an exorcist who confronted suffering and oppression in all its forms, a prophet who reached out to those pushed to the margins and fearlessly challenged those in authority. The Gospels make clear that it was because of the profound commitment of his mission and its challenge to destructive power that Jesus was condemned to crucifixion. Thus the cross stands as an indictment of injustice and suffering imposed on the innocent.

Jesus as Innocent

All four gospels clearly state that Jesus was innocent of the crimes for which he was formally accused. Mark, for example, notes that the plot to arrest and condemn Jesus must be forged in stealth and depends on betrayal (14:1-2). The testimony brought against Jesus before the Sanhedrin is branded as manifestly false:

> The chief priests and the whole Sanhedrin were looking for testimony against Jesus in order to put him to death, but they couldn't find any. Many brought false testimony against him, but they contradicted each other. Some stood to offer false witness against him, saying, "We heard him saying, 'I will destroy this temple, constructed by humans, and within three days I will build another, one not made by humans.'" But their testimonies didn't agree even on this point. (Mark 14:55-59)

Pilate, the Roman procurator, is reluctant to condemn Jesus because he surmises that the leaders had handed Jesus over "because of jealousy" (15:10), and therefore Pilate attempts futilely to exchange Jesus for Barabbas (15:6-15).

---

17. Note the essential conformity of gospel passion accounts to the creedal formula cited by Paul in 1 Cor 15:3-4: "Christ died for our sins in line with the scriptures, he was buried, and he rose on the third day in line with the scriptures."

17

Matthew's account is similar but he adds the testimony of Judas himself, who is stricken with remorse when Jesus is condemned and returns to the leaders the money he had received and confesses: "I did wrong because I betrayed an innocent man" (27:4). Another unique voice in Matthew's account is that of Pilate's wife, who warns her husband, "Leave that righteous man alone. I've suffered much today in a dream because of him" (27:19). In Matthew, Pilate is also emphatic about Jesus' innocence. Even as he cedes to the demands of Jesus' opponents, the Roman prefect reasserts his conviction that Jesus is innocent, washing his hands in view of the crowd and declaring, "I'm innocent of this man's blood.... It's your problem" (27:24).[18]

Luke's account also strongly affirms the innocence of Jesus. When first presented with the accusations against Jesus, Pilate flatly declares to the leaders and the crowds, "I find no legal basis for action against this man" (23:4). Luke adds the curious scene about Pilate sending Jesus to Herod Antipas, the ruler of lower Galilee, who was in Jerusalem for the festival (23:6-12). Even though Herod mocks Jesus and treats him as a fool, he concludes that he is innocent. After Jesus returns from Herod, Pilate's declaration of his innocence is even stronger: "You brought this man before me as one who was misleading the people. I have questioned him in your presence and found nothing in this man's conduct that provides a legal basis for the charges you have brought against him. Neither did Herod, because Herod returned him to us. He's done nothing that deserves death. Therefore, I'll have him whipped, then let him go" (23:14-17). The motif of Jesus' innocence carries through the remainder of Luke's Passion Narrative.[19] One of the criminals crucified alongside Jesus—a scene found only in Luke—adds his testimony: "We are rightly condemned, for we are receiving the appropriate sentence for what we did. But this man has done nothing wrong" (23:41).

The climactic declaration of innocence comes at the moment of Jesus' death when the centurion who stood guard at the cross praises God and testifies, "It's really true: this man was righteous" (Luke 23:47). The Greek word translated here as "righteous" is *dikaios*, meaning "just." Thus the centurion does not simply say that Jesus is "innocent" and has not committed any crime

18. Matthew's description of Pilate's gesture is actually reflective of Deut 21:8-9, a Jewish ritual gesture expressing innocence regarding the shedding of human blood; see Senior, *The Passion of Jesus in the Gospel of Matthew*, 116–22.

19. Some commentators on Luke conclude that this emphasis on Pilate's declaration of Jesus' innocence fits into an overall apologetic purpose of Luke–Acts: Roman authority itself declares that Jesus (and by implication the movement he inspires) is innocent of any crime. However, see Lee, "Pilate and the Crucifixion of Jesus in Luke–Acts," in *Luke–Acts and Empire*, ed. Rhoads, Esterline, and Lee, 84–106; and Rowe, *World Upside Down*—both of whom see Luke offering a subtle anti-Roman critique in his manner of portraying the role of Roman authorities.

warranting crucifixion but that he is, in fact, "just"—a man of integrity and virtue, the truth that makes the injustice of the punishment inflicted on Jesus all the more heinous. Luke, it should be noted, carries this idea of the innocence of the Crucified Jesus over into his account of the Acts of the Apostles. Reproaches for the death of the innocent Jesus appear in several of the speeches in Acts (see 2:23; 3:14-15; 4:28; 14:28).

John's Gospel, too, presents the crucifixion of Jesus as an act of injustice. As a prisoner before the high priest Annas, Jesus himself boldly declares his own innocence: "I've spoken openly to the world" and have taught "in synagogues and in the temple"; he had said nothing "in private" (18:20). When struck by one of the temple police because of his answer, Jesus challenges his attacker: "If I speak wrongly, testify about what was wrong. But if I speak correctly, why do you strike me?" (18:23). Pilate, too, repeatedly declares Jesus' innocence: "I find no grounds for any charge against him" (18:38). At the climax of Jesus' interrogation, Pilate brings Jesus, beaten and crowned with thorns, out in view of the crowd and once again declares his innocence: "Look! I'm bringing him out to you to let you know that I find no grounds for a charge against him" (19:4). Only after his repeated attempts to release Jesus fail does Pilate accede to the demands of the people (19:8-12).

The Gospels express more interest in the involvement of the Jewish religious leaders in the condemnation of Jesus than they do in that of the Roman authorities. The relationship of Jesus to Judaism and his innocence in that context was much more religiously compelling and needed explanation in the Jewish Christian context of early Christianity than the brutality of the Roman Empire, which could be taken for granted.[20] Yet, at the same time, the gospel narratives do not exonerate the Roman civil authority that ultimately puts Jesus to death. Pilate is presented as weak and vacillating. Even though he is convinced of the innocence of Jesus, he has him tortured and, out of expediency and concern for his own political position, gives way to the demands of the leaders and crowds and condemns Jesus to capital punishment. The overall portrait of the Roman procurator presented in the trial and condemnation of Jesus is one of a public official who is corrupt and utterly unjust.

Jesus the Healer and Exorcist: The Path to the Cross

While Jesus is innocent of the charges of blasphemy and sedition hurled at him in the Passion Narratives, the Gospels also note that Jesus' mission of

---

20. See the discussion and survey of literature in Senior, "Matthew at the Crossroads of Early Christianity," in *The Gospel of Matthew at the Crossroads of Early Christianity*, ed. Senior, 3–23.

19

healing and exorcism and his association with outcasts and sinners was a trigger for the deadly opposition that builds against him.

That Jesus was a healer and exorcist is strongly affirmed in all four gospels. The opening scenes of the Gospel of Mark present Jesus, imbued with the power of the Spirit at his baptism, plunging into a sea of pain and distress. His ministry begins with a public confrontation with the unclean spirit that torments the man in the synagogue of Capernaum. The demon is well aware of Jesus' mission to liberate humans from the grip of evil and suffering: "What have you to do with us, Jesus of Nazareth? Have you come to destroy us?" (Mark 1:24). That initial scene is followed by a stream of healings and exorcisms that fill the first twenty-four hours of Jesus' stay in Capernaum and continue throughout his Galilean ministry.

Healings and exorcisms are also integral to the portrayal of Jesus' ministry in Matthew and Luke. Matthew, for example, introduces the crowds of the sick and tormented who flock to Jesus from all points of the compass (4:23-25) as the preface to the Sermon on the Mount. Later, Matthew will collect a series of healing and exorcism stories in chapters 8–9, illustrating the twofold ministry of Jesus as teacher and healer (see 4:23; 9:35). Luke, too, begins Jesus' public ministry with a reference to his role as physician in the inaugural scene in the synagogue of Nazareth, with its evoking of the healing ministries of the great prophets Elijah and Elisha (4:23). Immediately following this dramatic scene in Nazareth, Luke portrays Jesus as plunging into a series of healings and exorcisms. John's Gospel, too, portrays Jesus as healer through a series of signs that extend throughout the public ministry of Jesus, climaxing with the raising of Lazarus in chapter 11.[21] Unlike the Synoptic Gospels, John does not emphasize Jesus' role as exorcist, yet, as we will note, the power of Satan lurks behind the opposition to Jesus and will emerge as the driving force for Judas's betrayal.[22]

From the perspective of the Gospels, the boundary between healing and exorcisms is permeable since ultimately the root of all human suffering is the power of death and evil.[23] The worldview of biblical Judaism and the New Testament itself is that there is an intrinsic link between sickness, sin, death, and the demonic. Mortality was ultimately rooted in the force of evil. The basic pattern is set with the opening chapters of the creation accounts in Genesis. God creates the world to be intrinsically good and beautiful but hu-

---

21. On the function of the Lazarus story as a summation of Jesus' mission; see below, pp. 66–67.

22. See, e.g., John 8:44-51. See below, pp. 22–23, 68–69 concerning role of Satan in the passion story.

23. See, e.g., Garrett, *The Demise of the Devil.*

mans rebel against God and bring into the world of beauty and goodness the specter of mortality and evil. This fundamental perspective is put in poetic form in the opening chapter of the Wisdom of Solomon:

> Don't seek death through the error of your ways. Don't invite destruction on yourself by what you do. God didn't make death. God takes no delight in the ruin of anything that lives. God created everything so that it might exist. The creative forces at work in the cosmos are life-giving. There is no destructive poison in them. The underworld doesn't rule on earth. Doing what is right means living forever.
>
> In spite of this, the ungodly called out to death by what they did and said. Thinking that death was their friend, they lost their resolve and made a treaty with death. Let them have each other: death and the ungodly belong together! (1:12-16)

It is important to underscore that the gospel link between suffering and evil does not imply that the person who is sick or suffering is thereby personally culpable. The assertion sometimes made by well-intentioned but misinformed people of faith is that if one is sick or has some form of suffering it is caused by a lack of faith or some personal sin. This is not representative of sound Christian thought and faith. As the book of Job affirms, there is in fact *innocent* suffering.[24] Some suffering we can bring on ourselves: a habit of smoking can ruin our health; a poor diet can lead to a heart attack; irresponsible building construction can lead to a catastrophic collapse. But the perspective illustrated in the gospel stories of healing and exorcism is working on a different level: the very fact that humans are vulnerable to sickness and death itself is a symptom of our mortality, a mortality that in the biblical perspective is ultimately caused not by God but by the force of evil that has introduced the specter of suffering and death into the beauty of God's creation.

Thus the Gospels leave no doubt that one of the primary expressions of Jesus' mission was to alleviate human suffering and to lift away the burden that evil had imposed on human beings. This was also expressed in Jesus' compassionate association with sinners and outcasts. Jesus earns the hostility of the leaders by calling Levi as a disciple and then by dining with the tax collector and his friends: "Why is he eating with sinners and tax collectors?" (Mark 2:16). Luke, too, notes that Jesus' association with these unsavory types prompted the leaders to grumble: "This man welcomes sinners and eats with them" (15:1-2). In Matthew 11:16-19, Jesus confronts his opponents who characterize him as "a glutton and a drunk, a friend of tax collectors

---

24. See the reflections of Gutierrez, *On Job.*

21

and sinners." Matthew cites Isaiah 53:4 as a sign that Jesus' mission of healing and exorcism fulfills the will of God expressed in the scriptures: "That
evening people brought to Jesus many who were demon-possessed. He threw
the spirits out with just a word. He healed everyone who was sick. This hap-
pened so that what Isaiah the prophet said would be fulfilled: *He is the one
who took our illnesses and carried away our diseases*" (8:16-17). The experience
of opposing suffering and lifting away the burden of pain and oppression is,
in fact, the embodiment of what the Gospels mean by "God's kingdom" (see
Matt 12:28; Luke 11:20).

The Gospels link this healing and inclusive ministry of Jesus with his
death on the cross. Precisely because of these characteristic actions of Jesus,
the plot to kill him gets underway (Mark 3:6). What is viewed as transgressions by Jesus' opponents is clearly seen by the gospel as the manifestation of
the reign of God coming to fruition in the ministry of Jesus.

The Confrontation with Ultimate Evil

The Gospels affirm another ominous cause of Jesus' death on the cross.
Lurking behind the human opposition to Jesus is the influence of ultimate evil.
That Jesus confronts the power of death and evil is manifest in his ministry of
exorcism. The Gospels go on to assert that the demons, proponents of death
who oppose Jesus as the giver of life, have a hand in his death on the cross.

This is explicit in the Gospel of Luke. At the conclusion of the temptation story, where the demon attempts to lure Jesus away from his God-given
mission, Luke notes, "After finishing every temptation, the devil departed
from him until the next opportunity" (4:13). The words "next opportunity"
translate the Greek word *kairos*, implying a significant future moment when
the assault of evil on Jesus will resume.

Although Jesus will confront the demonic in several exorcism stories
throughout the gospel,[25] the supreme moment gets underway at the beginning of Luke's Passion Narrative. While the religious leaders were "looking
for a way to kill Jesus" (22:2), that opportunity presents itself in the person of
Judas who offers to betray Jesus. Luke explicitly notes, "Then Satan entered
Judas, called Iscariot, who was one of the Twelve. He went out and discussed
with the chief priests and the officers of the temple guard how he could hand
Jesus over to them" (22:3-4). After his meeting with the religious leaders,
Luke ominously notes, "He [Judas] agreed and began looking for an oppor-
tunity to hand Jesus over to them—a time when the crowds would be absent"

25. Luke 4:33-37; 8:26-39; 11:14-15, 18; 13:16. In 10:17-19, Jesus exults with his disciples that
Satan had fallen "from heaven like lightning."

(22:6). The same root word—*kairos* or "opportune time"—is used here as in the temptation account, clearly indicating that Luke's Gospel sees continuity between the opening assault of the demonic on Jesus at the beginning of his mission and its climax in the decision to put Jesus to death engineered by Judas and the religious leaders. This is reinforced in Jesus' words at the moment of his arrest, as Judas, now under the sway of the demonic, leads a crowd into the place where Jesus is praying on the slopes of the Mount of Olives: "This is your time, when darkness rules" (Luke 22:53). As Jesus' death approaches Luke will note that "darkness covered the whole earth . . . while the sun stopped shining" (23:44-45).

John's Gospel, too, points to the demonic as a driving force behind the crucifixion of Jesus. Here, too, the figure of Judas who betrays Jesus becomes an instrument in Satan's hand. At the beginning of the last discourse, Jesus solemnly turns his attention to the impending moment of his death: "Before the Festival of Passover, Jesus knew that his time [literally in the Greek, "his hour"] had come to leave this world and go to the Father. Having loved his own who were in the world, he loved them fully. . . . The devil had already provoked Judas, Simon Iscariot's son, to betray Jesus" (13:1-2). The drama continues when, after the scene of Jesus washing the feet of his disciples, he begins to foretell his impending betrayal. Judas, the one with whom Jesus shares a piece of bread, is identified as the betrayer. The gospel notes, "After Judas took the bread, Satan entered into him. Jesus told him, 'What you are about to do, do quickly'" (13:27). The scene concludes with Judas's departure to carry out his betrayal: "So when Judas took the bread, he left immediately. And it was night" (13:30). The reference to "night," along with John's characteristic description of Jesus' death as the "hour," "time" (see, for example, 12:27; 13:1), aligns John's account with that of Luke at this point.

The Gospels therefore affirm that lurking behind the crucifixion of Jesus is the power of "darkness"—the power of ultimate evil that stands diametrically opposed to the power of life embodied in Jesus himself. Thus the cross itself illustrates the power of ultimate evil and death that seems to holds humanity in its grip and is inflicted through injustice and oppression.

III. The Cross as Paradox and the Spirituality of Lament

The cross as symbol of innocent suffering and of injustice poses a challenge to faith. The question is raised over and over in human history: Why? Why do the innocent suffer? Why the death of a child? Why the abomination of the Shoah and other genocides throughout history? Why does injustice so often seem to prevail? How does faith in a God of love and compassion and mercy square with the reality of such suffering?[26]

The Bible itself is no stranger to these wrenching questions. The book of Job challenges easy answers to the reason for suffering, rejecting the explanation that only the guilty suffer.[27] The Wisdom of Solomon takes note of the suffering of the innocent, just man and wrestles with other experiences that cry to heaven for explanation—the death of the young, the prosperity of the wicked, the shame of sterility (see particularly Wis 2–5). Paul, too, did not hesitate to enumerate his sufferings, as in the litany of 2 Corinthians 11:21-30, and the puzzle they posed for him. While refusing to give in to despair he nevertheless confesses to "experiencing all kinds of trouble...confused...harassed...knocked down," carrying Jesus' death around in his body (2 Cor 4:8-10).

One of the biblical prayer forms associated with the crucifixion of Jesus is the lament and here too, in this striking expression of biblical faith, one can also see the Bible's own struggle with the challenge of innocent suffering caused by injustice and persecution. Prayers of lament can be found throughout the biblical literature but take on a more discernible form in the psalms. Laments are prayers characterized by raw emotion, by daring challenges to God in the midst of suffering, and by vivid expressions of anger and confusion directed at God and wrung from the heart of one who suffers yet still prays.[28]

One of the most powerful expressions of the lament prayer form is Psalm 22, a psalm that had a profound influence on the shape and tone of the Passion Narratives, particularly those of Mark and Matthew. Psalm 22 has a characteristic format found in many examples of biblical lament; what begins as an inventory of suffering concludes with a sudden rush of praise and thanksgiving. The first half of Psalm 22 is pure lament, beginning with the dramatic first verse that is found on the lips of the dying Jesus in the passion accounts of Mark and Matthew: "My God! My God, why have you left me all alone?" The lament that follows through verse 21 is a wrenching soliloquy of pain and isolation by one who seems to be in terrible psychological isolation, surrounded by torment. ("Why are you so far from saving me—so far from my anguished groans?" [v. 1]). The psalmist's suffering is extreme and results

26. See the variety of theological reflections on the meaning of suffering constructed over the ages in Ryan, *God and the Mystery of Human Suffering*; see also Harrington, *Why Do We Suffer?*.

27. See Ryan, *God and the Mystery of Human Suffering*, 34–42.

28. On the theology of lament, see Waltke, Houston, and Moore, *The Psalms as Christian Lament*; also, Brueggemann, "The Costly Loss of Lament": 57–71; Simundson, *Faith under Fire*, 43–61.

in a cry to God: "My God, I cry out during the day, but you don't answer; even at nighttime I don't stop" (v. 2).

One particular suffering in the list of laments is noteworthy. In verses 7-8, the enemies of the psalmist mock him and, "shaking their heads," say, "He committed himself to the LORD, so let God rescue him; let God deliver him because God likes him so much." This verse is also found in the Wisdom of Solomon (2:18), cataloguing the sufferings of the just one who is assaulted by mockers and evildoers for his trust in God. This same verse will be explicitly cited by Matthew's Passion Narrative as the gospel describes those who mock Jesus as he hangs on the cross (27:43). The entire scene of mockery found in Mark (15:29-32) and Matthew (27:39-44) echoes both Psalm 22 and the mockery of the just man in Wisdom 2–5.

The lament of Psalm 22 reaches its greatest intensity in verses 19-21:

But you, LORD! Don't be far away!
    You are my strength!
    Come quick and help me!
Deliver me from the sword.
    Deliver my life from the power of the dog.
    Save me from the mouth of the lion.
    From the horns of the wild oxen
    you have answered me!

At this point in the psalm the mood changes without explanation into a hymn of exuberant praise for God's deliverance. "From the horns of the wild oxen you have answered me!" (v. 21). "Because he [God] didn't despise or detest the suffering of the one who suffered—he didn't hide his face from me. No, he listened when I cried out to him for help" (v. 24). God's deliverance of the one who suffered and cried to him leads to a string of praises: "I will declare your name to my brothers and sisters; I will praise you in the very center of the congregation! All of you who revere the LORD—praise him!" (vv. 22-23). Praise for the greatness of God and thankfulness for his trustworthiness will even extend to whole world: "Every part of the earth will remember and come back to the LORD; every family among all the nations will worship you" (v. 27). The ecstasy of the psalmist leads him to affirm that even those in Sheol will praise God! "Indeed, all the earth's powerful will worship him; all who are descending to the dust will kneel before him; my being also lives for him" (v. 29). Future generations, too, will praise God for his fidelity: "Future descendants will serve him; generations to come will be told about my Lord.

They will proclaim God's righteousness to those not yet born, telling them what God has done" (vv. 30-31).

No explanation is given for this startling move from darkest lament to exuberant praise. Perhaps the lament itself is a kind of catharsis, a raw form of prayer, directed to God with strong emotion and uninhibited language. The outpouring of one's pain and confusion to a seemingly absent God leads paradoxically to a deeper sense of God's abiding presence. As will be amplified in the Passion Narrative of Matthew, who draws heavily on Psalm 22, the underlying concern of this lament psalm is with God's "trustworthiness."[29] In the midst of inexplicable suffering and isolation, is God present?

Paradoxically this rich and powerful prayer form found in the Old Testament finds a place in the New Testament primarily on the lips of Jesus as he faces death on the cross. A first example is the gospel tradition of Jesus' intense prayer on the eve of his passion. Each of the evangelists leaves his particular stamp on this account. For Matthew and Mark the scene takes place in the olive grove of Gethsemane, on the slopes of the Mount of Olives, as Jesus returns from the Last Supper to go to Bethany where he is residing. Luke notes that Jesus goes to a place on "the Mount of Olives" (22:39). Here, Jesus prays repeatedly and with anguish to be delivered from death. He tells his disciples, "My soul is sorrowful even to the point of death, remain here and stay awake" (Mark 14:34 AT; Matt 26:38). Mark's version of the prayer captures its profound spirit both of anguish in the face of death and fidelity to God's will: "Abba, Father, for you all things are possible. Take this cup of suffering away from me. However—not what I want but what you want" (Mark 14:36).

Luke has a somewhat different format. Like an athlete steeling himself for an impending contest of strength, Jesus is in *agōnia* (a term often used to describe the exertion of the athlete before a contest) and sweats profusely (as if in blood); an angel appears to strengthen him as he faces the terrible "test" of death (see Luke 22:39-46). At the Last Supper, Luke's Jesus warned his disciples about the assault of evil that was about to befall them, and he repeats that warning here (see 22:40, "Pray that you won't give in to temptation").[30] John does not include this prayer in his Passion Narrative but seems to have transposed his version to the anguished soliloquy of Jesus in 12:27: "Now I

---

29. See below, pp. 46–50.

30. Luke's Passion Narrative emphasizes the issue of the apostles' perseverance through the test that evil will inflict on them, reflecting Luke's concern to have the apostles be the link between the mission of Jesus in the gospel and the continuation of that mission in Acts. On this, see S. Brown, *Apostasy and Perseverance in the Theology of Luke*; also John T. Carroll, "The Death of Jesus in the Gospel according to Luke," in Carroll and Green, *The Death of Jesus in Early Christianity*, 74–77.

am deeply troubled. What should I say? 'Father, save me from this time [literally "hour"]'? No, for this is the reason I have come to this time."[31] Many interpreters also believe that the Letter to the Hebrews also reflects the Gethsemane tradition: "During his days on earth, Christ offered prayers and requests with loud cries and tears as his sacrifices to the one who was able to save him from death. He was heard because of his godly devotion" (Heb 5:7).[32]

Cutting across all of these versions is the affirmation that Jesus, faced with the specter of death and all that it meant for his mission, cries out to God for deliverance. In the face of impending and unjust suffering, Jesus laments.

Both Mark and Matthew follow through with the spirit of lament in their description of the final moments of Jesus' life. Echoes of Psalm 22 are close to the surface in both accounts: the soldiers cast lots for Jesus' garments (Ps 22:18; Mark 15:22; Matt 27:35); Jesus is surrounded by hostile mockers (Ps 22:7-8, 12-13, 16; Mark 15:27-32; Matt 27:38-43). Matthew makes the parallel explicit when in 27:43 he quotes Psalm 22:8, "He trusts in God, so let God deliver him now if he wants to. He said, 'I'm God's Son.'" And both evangelists portray Jesus' final words as the first verse of Psalm 22:1, "My God, my God why have you left me?" (see Mark 15:34; Matt 27:46). Interpreters debate whether in citing the first verse of the psalm, the evangelists mean to invoke the entire psalm—that is, Jesus' final prayer not only includes the psalm's stark opening words of lament and near despair but also the affirmation of trust in God's deliverance that permeates the entire psalm.[33] In any case, it is this first verse that becomes the words of the dying Jesus; Matthew makes that even more explicit when he seems to have Jesus repeat the words of the psalm at the very moment he expires.[34] The Gospels of Mark and Matthew, therefore, give full expression to the motif we are illustrating: in the face of the injustice of Jesus' suffering and death, one can only lament and cry out to God in distress.

Neither evangelist, however, leaves the situation there; in both accounts the abject horror of Jesus' death is followed immediately by a strong affirmation of God's vindication of Jesus' suffering even before the account

---

31. John, however, situates the subsequent arrest of Jesus in a location that harmonizes with that of the Synoptics. Jesus goes to a "garden" on the other side of the "Kidron valley"—the valley that separates the temple area from the Mount of Olives (18:1).

32. See McCruden, "The Eloquent Blood of Jesus," esp. 514–17.

33. See the balanced view in Donahue and Harrington, *The Gospel of Mark*, 450–52.

34. In contrast to Mark's version, Matthew uses the verb *kraxas* ("to cry out"), which is repeatedly used in the LXX version of Ps 22 and adds the word *palin* ("again"), suggesting that Jesus repeats the prayer of 27:46 as he dies. See further, Senior, *The Passion of Jesus in the Gospel of Matthew*, 139–40.

of the empty tomb and the proclamation of Jesus' resurrection. In Mark's account, the temple veil is torn in two and the centurion who witnessed Jesus' death acclaims him as the Son of God (Mark 15:38-39). In Matthew the signs of vindication are even more dramatic: The temple veil is torn asunder, the earth quakes, the tombs are opened, and the bodies of the "holy people" are raised—apocalyptic signs that prompt the centurion and his companions to acclaim Jesus as Son of God (Matt 27:51-54).[35] If Jesus' final prayer is one both of lament at the injustice of death and of trust in God's deliverance, the Gospels want to affirm that trust is not in vain.

Conclusion

While for his opponents, the condemnation of Jesus of Nazareth to crucifixion represented the ultimate rejection of Jesus and his mission, for Christians Jesus' suffering death on the cross gives new meaning to the experience of human suffering. Thus the cross, from the perspective of Christian faith, symbolizes a variety of powerful realities. Jesus dies on the cross and therefore his genuine humanity is unconditionally affirmed. Because Jesus, God's own Son, also faced abject suffering, the Christian is able to find meaning even in the midst of suffering and loss. Yet, at the same time, the fierce commitment of Jesus to heal and overcome the evils that afflict humanity guides the followers of Jesus to first oppose and alleviate human suffering in all its forms; death, as Paul declared, is the "last enemy" (1 Cor 15:26). The death of Jesus on the cross also makes it a symbol of opposition to all unjust suffering and oppression afflicted on the vulnerable, an evil that the Gospels ultimately judge as demonic. Like the Crucified Jesus, the Christian is to confront and alleviate all human suffering. And finally, the Gospels, drawing on the rich heritage of Judaism, make room for the paradox of human suffering and the searing questions it poses, allowing the faithful followers of Jesus to lament the reality of suffering and to search for God and the meaning of suffering in their moments of darkness.

---

35. These signs evoke the scene of the dry bones in Ezek 37:11-14 as well as the reference to the opening of graves in Dan 12:1-2 and may also reflect the continuing influence of Ps 22 on Matthew's account. Even those who are "descending to the dust will kneel" (Ps 22:29) and "every family among all the nations will worship you" (Ps 22:27). On this see Senior, *The Passion of Jesus in the Gospel of Matthew*, 141–57; see also Senior, "The Death of Jesus and the Resurrection of the Holy Ones, Matthew 27:51-53."

Chapter Three

The Cross and Salvation

A constant and deep conviction of Christian faith is that through the death of Jesus on the cross we have been saved from our sins. The cross of Christ is both the symbol of our salvation and the means through which salvation has come. Yet explaining how it is that the death of Jesus on the cross saves us from sin and death is no simple matter, and the New Testament itself, along with subsequent Christian tradition, has struggled to find a clear and coherent explanation of what faith in the efficacy of the cross unconditionally affirms. In what way can the death of Jesus on the cross save human beings from their sins?

It is not a question of falling mute before this mystery of faith; on the contrary, the New Testament itself and Christian theology have brought forth a rich variety of metaphors, analogies, and theological constructs in an attempt to illumine this mystery. Our goal here is not to attempt to recapitulate the whole of Christian theology on this point but, in the spirit of this series, to explore some of the key New Testament texts that reflect on the saving power of the cross of Christ.

I. Essential Assumptions

The Resurrection

Before turning to specific texts, there are some key assumptions about the meaning of the cross as a source and sign of salvation that need to be kept in mind. First and foremost is that, from the perspective of Christian faith, Jesus' death on the cross is essentially linked to his resurrection from the dead. Without the victory of resurrection, the crucifixion of Jesus becomes another unjust and tragic execution, one in a long string of such tragedies in human history. In the case of Jesus, the tragedy would be compounded because a most graceful human being, a wise teacher, a powerful healer, a strong prophet, and a compassionate friend of those in need had his life senselessly struck down by powerful forces arrayed against him. Add to that the Christian claim that this Jesus is the Messiah, the promised Redeemer of the world, and the stakes are raised much higher. If the death of Jesus was the end of the story, perhaps he would have been remembered with reverence and sadness by his close friends and followers. Jesus of Nazareth would take his place with other great human beings whose lives were tragically cut short, but no one would be tempted to affirm that his life brought salvation to the world. The ancient world was familiar with the motif of the "noble death"—examples where heroic teachers or soldiers or civic leaders would sacrifice their lives for a good cause or for the nation or for the common good. Such noble deaths could be inspiring, advance a cause, and leave an imprint in human memory, but no claim would be made that such a death saved humanity from the power of sin and death.

The death of Jesus on the cross takes on a very different and profound meaning because it is not the end of the story—the one who suffered the cruel death of crucifixion is, in the fundamental conviction of Christian faith, also the one whom the power of God liberates from death through resurrection. Without this link between death and resurrection, Christian faith in the efficacy of the cross could not begin. The Apostle Paul speaks bluntly of this as he wrestles with the meaning of resurrection in his First Letter to the Corinthians:

> If there's no resurrection of the dead, then Christ hasn't been raised either. If Christ hasn't been raised, then our preaching is useless and your faith is useless. We are found to be false witnesses about God, because we testified against God that he raised Christ, when he didn't raise him if it's the case that the dead aren't raised. If the dead aren't raised then Christ hasn't been raised either. If Christ hasn't been raised, then your faith is worthless; you are still in your sins, and what's more, those who have died in Christ are gone forever. If we have a hope in Christ only in this life, then we deserve to be pitied more than anyone else. (1 Cor 15:13-19)

Thus the saving power of Jesus' death on the cross is essentially linked to the outcome of his being raised from the dead. That conviction is expressed in multiple ways even within the final chapters of the gospel accounts: The tomb is empty, various witnesses encounter the Risen Christ, abject sorrow and despair turn into ecstasy and joy, a spirit of listless defeat on the part of the disciples is replaced with conviction and energy, their mission, which they had abandoned in betrayal and fear, is now renewed. It is on this experiential basis of a profound transformation from death to life that the various New Testament writings produce their reflections on the saving power of the cross.

The Cross of Jesus as the Ultimate Expression of His Mission

For the cross of Christ to be seen as both sign and means of salvation, there is another assumption that needs to be taken into account. As noted previously, the Gospels portray the death of Jesus on the cross as the final expression of his mission.[1] Jesus, in effect, dies because of the way he lives. Jesus' characteristic actions of healing and exorcisms, his association with sinners and the marginalized, his interpretation of the law concerning Sabbath observance and cultic purity, and his prophetic condemnations of what he judged to be hypocrisy or injustice—all of these are met with opposition that ultimately climaxes in the condemnation of Jesus by the religious authorities and the execution of Jesus by the Romans. Thus the crucifixion of Jesus is not portrayed as an unanticipated tragedy that breaks into the gospel drama without preparation or warning. It is, rather, the final and most definitive statement of Jesus' commitment to giving his life for others—a self-transcendence and act of service already evident throughout his public ministry. Thus the saving significance of the cross of Jesus finds meaning, in part, through the character and commitment of his life.

This emphasis on the cross of Christ as the ultimate expression of his mission has become an important note in current theology.[2] For some, a theology of the cross that appears to be isolated from the ministry of Jesus can distort the Christian message and reduce it to a drama in which God seems to arbitrarily deliver Jesus to a cruel death in order to atone for sin or to exact a payment for humanity's debt of sin. The cross can become a kind of theological shorthand whose full message, when teased out, leaves Christian theology with an image of a God who is cruel and vindictive, exacting the death of God's own son as payment for human failure or to avenge God's honor. At the same time, the purpose of Jesus' life can be interpreted solely as a march to death rather than a mission to bring life.

1. See earlier, pp. 19–23.
2. See "Introduction: Why the Cross?," pp. xiii–xviii.

Both of these dimensions—the outcome of resurrection and the connection to Jesus' ministry—need to be at work in constructing a theology of the cross. The mission of Jesus allows his death on the cross to be understood as an act of self-transcendence for the sake of the other, as a *diakonia* or profound service that brings life to others, as an act of consummate love expressed in the willingness to give one's life for the beloved. Jesus' resurrection from the dead lifts this act of service and love to a unique level of meaning and consequence—affirming that the God of the scriptures and the God of Christian faith is not a vindictive or an arbitrary death-dealing potentate but a God who is life giving and whose love for humanity knows no bounds.

II. The Saving Power of the Cross in the Synoptic Gospels

The affirmation of the saving power of the cross is affirmed in a variety of ways in the Synoptic Gospels.

The Gospel of Mark

The Gospel of Mark draws a straight line between the messianic mission of Jesus and the meaning of his death on the cross. Jesus' characteristic actions of healing, of associating with tax collectors and sinners, and of interpreting the cultic laws with an emphasis on mercy and compassion earn the anger of the religious leaders, who begin a plot to destroy him (Mark 3:6).[3] So hostile is the opposition to Jesus and his liberating mission that he is accused of being in league with Satan and his exorcisms carried out through the power of evil—an accusation that in the perspective of Mark's portrayal of Jesus is as far from the truth as possible (see 3:22-30). The reader of the gospel has already witnessed that the power that animates Jesus, the Christ and the Son of God, is God's own spirit (1:9-11) and that the reign Jesus' mission comes to enact is not the rule of Beelzebul, the "ruler of the demons," (as his opponents claim in 3:22) but the reign of God (1:14-15). That hostility comes to a full boil when Jesus has a final series of encounters with his opponents in the temple precinct and will lead to the leaders' final decision to have Jesus destroyed (see Mark 11:18; 14:1-2).

---

3. See earlier, p. 19–32.

Mark 10:45: "The Human One didn't come to be served but rather to serve and to give his life to liberate many people."

The link between Jesus' messianic mission of liberating humans from the power of evil and his death on the cross is made explicit in Mark's Gospel in two key passages. The first is Jesus' saying in 10:45, "For the Human One [literally "the Son of Man"] didn't come to be served but rather to serve and to give his life to liberate many people" (literally "as a ransom for many"). The saying appears in the context of the third and final passion prediction made by Jesus in the course of his journey to Jerusalem and is part of his response to the aggressive ambition of the sons of Zebedee.[4] Their seeking places of honor—"one on your right and the other on your left when you enter your glory"—provokes the envious anger of the rest of the disciples but is met with Jesus' instruction on what authentic power means in the reign of God. The rulers among the Gentiles are tyrants who abuse their authority and lord it over others. But for the followers of Jesus true greatness is expressed not in status seeking but in service of others and in a spirit of humility (10:42-44). This spirit of life-giving service (*diakonia*) is the true meaning of Jesus' own giving of his life; the Son of Man came "not to be served but rather to serve" (*diakonēsai*), that is, "to give his life to liberate many people [literally: "as a ransom for the many"]." Thus this saying of Jesus at a climatic point in the gospel makes the death of Jesus equivalent to "serving"; the "ransom" (*lytron*) of his life that Jesus pays is, in fact, his self-transcending giving of life to others.

This saying of Jesus provides an important interpretation of the saving power of his death. The imagery used is that of a "ransom" (*lytron*) or "payment"; Jesus gives his "life" (*psyche*) "for the many" (*anti pollōn*); the term *many* here is equivalent to "all." The word for *ransom* used in this saying of Jesus has a variety of meanings, such as a payment for redeeming a captive or slave or a sacrifice made to liberate others, such as the sacrifice of their lives on the part of the Maccabeean martyrs.[5] It appears to be equivalent to the Greek term *apolytrōsis* or "ransom" or "redemption" found in Paul and other New Testament texts.[6]

---

4. Mark's Gospel sets a pattern: After each of the three passion predictions, one or more of the disciples express a counterview to which Jesus himself responds with discipleship instruction—see Peter in Mark 8:31-38; the disciples in 9:30-37; and the sons of Zebedee in 10:32-45.

5. See the discussion of the variety of meanings found in the biblical literature in Collins, *Mark*, 500.

6. See, e.g., Rom 3:24; 1 Cor 1:30; Eph 1:7, 14; 4:30; Heb 9:15; 11:35. See further, F. Danker, ed., *A Greek-English Lexicon of the New Testament and Other Christian Literature*, 3rd ed. (Chicago: University of Chicago Press, 2000), 117.

Many interpreters find in this saying of Jesus an echo of the Suffering Servant song in Isaiah 53:12, although in the Septuagint version of this passage the Greek word "ransom" (*lytron*) does not appear. There are a number of intriguing links between the New Testament portrayal of Jesus' sufferings and Isaiah's description of this mysterious representative figure (the king?) who suffers on behalf of Israel: "He was despised and avoided by others; a man who suffered, who knew sickness well" (Isa 53:3); "It was certainly our sickness that he carried, and our sufferings that he bore" (53:4); "He was pierced because of our rebellions and crushed because of our crimes" (53:5). The notion of giving one's life for others will also appear in Jesus' words over the bread and wine at the Last Supper (Mark 14:22-25). However, the full text of Isaiah also presents the Servant as a kind of "scapegoat" who has to bear the sin and guilt of the people: "He bore the punishment that made us whole; by his wounds we are healed. Like sheep we had all wandered away, each going its own way, but the LORD let fall on him all our crimes" (Isa 53:5-6). There is no clear echo of this motif in Mark's portrayal.

Much more compelling is the link Mark makes with the notion of service. The instruction to the disciples contrasts the brutalizing and oppressive power of the Gentile rulers (the Romans? the Herodians?) with that of Jesus, who is not arrogant or self-seeking but gives his life for the sake of the other. The healing power of Jesus that enables him to confront the power of evil that overwhelms God's people through illness and death paradoxically will find its ultimate expression on the cross where Jesus will give his very life for the sake of others.

Mark 14:22-25: The Final Passover

Another key text for Mark's interpretation of the death of Jesus is his account of the final Passover meal of Jesus and his disciples in 14:22-25.[7] While discussion of the meaning of this passage is often about its function as an "institution account" for the Christian Eucharist, its role within the Passion Narrative serves as a final passion prediction. Jesus' words and actions at the Passover meal reveal the meaning of the death he is about to experience.

The evangelist clearly interprets this final meal as a Passover meal; in 14:12-16 Jesus instructs two of his disciples to go into the city and to arrange for a place: "Where is my guest room where I can eat the Passover meal with my disciples?" (14:14). While Mark does not seem to emphasize this motif as much as will be the case with the Gospels of Luke and John, the Passover's

---

7. For a detailed commentary on the scene, see Senior, *The Passion of Jesus in the Gospel of Mark*, 53–62.

meaning as a liturgical recall of the redemptive exodus forms part of the backdrop of the scene.

The scene begins with Jesus' blessing over the bread: "While they were eating, Jesus took bread, blessed it, broke it, and gave it to them, and said, 'Take; this is my body'" (14:22). The presence of bread and Jesus' gestures of blessing it, breaking it, and distributing it to his disciples immediately recall the previous feeding stories in Mark's Gospel (see 6:34-44 and 8:1-10).[8]

"Bread" (*artos*) is a key symbol in the Gospel of Mark that expresses the entirety of Jesus' messianic mission. When Jesus declares, "It isn't right to take the children's bread [*artos*] and toss it to the dogs," the Syro-Phoenician woman counters by reminding Jesus that even the dogs eat the crumbs that fall from the children's table! (7:27-28). The feeding stories themselves express in vivid practical terms the ultimate purpose of Jesus' work as Messiah—out of compassion to feed those who "were like sheep without a shepherd" (6:34; and similarly in 8:2 where Jesus notes that the crowds "have nothing to eat"). It is this mission of feeding both Jew and Gentile with the one bread that the chronically dull disciples of Mark's Gospel fail to grasp (see 6:52 and 8:17-21). When the disciples are unable to absorb the meaning of Jesus' walking on the water, the gospel notes, "That's because they hadn't understood about the loaves. Their hearts had been changed so that they resisted God's ways" (6:52). The ultimate significance of the "bread" in Mark is made clear at the final Passover meal. Here Jesus identifies the bread "broken" and "given" as his own body that will be "broken" on the cross of death. All of the giving of life that had characterized his mission until now comes to its climactic point as Jesus gives his own body for the sake of those in need.

The words over the cup have a similar meaning. In conjunction with his third passion prediction, Jesus had asked the sons of Zebedee if they were able to "drink the cup [*potērion*] I drink" (10:38)—a clear reference to his death.[9] And in Jesus' final prayer in Gethsemane, he will ask his father to "take this cup [*potērion*] of suffering away from me" (14:36), an intense prayer asking God to deliver him from death. Now at the Passover meal, Jesus takes a "cup," gives thanks, and gives it to his disciples to drink. Again, the words of Jesus become an interpretation of the meaning of his death: "This is the blood of the covenant, which is poured out for many" (14:24). The reference to "blood" and "covenant" evoke Exodus 24, where Moses takes the blood of sacrificed oxen and sprinkles the blood both on the altar and on the Israelites

---

8. The two feeding stories in Mark, with their wilderness setting, recall the manna (Exod 16:1-36) as well as similar stories in the prophets Elijah and Elisha (1 Kgs 17:8-16 and 2 Kgs 4:42-44).

9. See Collins, *Mark*, 496–97. Collins surmises that the "cup" evokes the "cup of divine wrath" in Isa 57:17 and Jer 25:15-39, implying the death that Jesus would endure.

themselves and declares, "This is the blood of the covenant that the LORD now makes with you on the basis of all these words" (Exod 24:8). The blood of Jesus to be shed on the cross renews the covenant of God with his people; it is Jesus' own death ("*my* blood")—a death that is the culminating act of service on the part of Jesus that is ultimately expressive of God's care for his people and God's purpose for the messianic mission of Jesus. The outpouring of the blood of Jesus is not presented as the price to be paid to appease God's wrath but as the definitive expression of God's intent to radically defeat the power of death and to bring new life to humanity.

This highly charged scene concludes with Jesus' words: "I assure you that I won't drink wine again until that day when I drink it in a new way in God's kingdom" (14:25). Here in a sense is another passion prediction; both dimensions of the paschal mystery are reflected here in language expressive of the Passover meal context. Jesus "won't drink wine again" with his disciples because the power of death will strike at him, the culmination of all of the hostility that had confronted his mission in the gospel. Underneath that opposition lurked the power of sin and death, and on the cross it would make its final assault. But because of the resurrection this would not be the final Passover—Jesus would "drink it in a new way in God's kingdom" (14:25b). God's life-giving power would defeat death and Jesus would celebrate the ultimate liberation feast with his disciples in the kingdom of God.

Mark 15:21-41: The Crucifixion of Jesus—God's Power Revealed in Weakness

Another text that is key for Mark's interpretation of the death of Jesus is the crucifixion scene itself. The actual moment of nailing Jesus to the cross is told with restraint: "It was nine in the morning when they crucified him" (15:25).[10]

A first significant indicator of Mark's intent is the mockery directed at Jesus by passersby, by the chief priests and scribes, and even by the two bandits crucified next to him. The inclusion of mockery directed at Jesus in the midst of his suffering reflects the influence both of Psalm 22 and the portrayal of the suffering just man in the Wisdom of Solomon on the passion story.[11]

Jesus is first mocked for his alleged threats against the temple: "Ha! So you were going to destroy the temple and rebuild it in three days, were you?"

10. This is true of all four gospels. Unlike the vivid and bloody portrayals found in art and, most recently, in Mel Gibson's 2004 film *The Passion of Christ*, the Gospels themselves leave out any detailed description of Jesus' physical torment. In this sense, they reflect the kind of restraint found in most Greco-Roman literature when referring to crucifixion, most likely because the horror of this act needed no elaboration. On this see Hengel, *Crucifixion*, 37–38.

11. See the earlier discussion of these texts, pp. 23–28.

(15:29)—recalling the accusation during the hearing before the council of religious leaders, an accusation that Mark clearly brands as false and contradictory (see 14:57-59). The connection of the temple with the death of Jesus will reappear with the tearing of the temple veil at the moment Jesus dies (15:38).[12] But more significant at this point are the words of mockery that are presented as a challenge to Jesus' supposed messianic power: "Save yourself and come down from that cross!" (15:30). This challenge of those who pass by is repeated with some elaboration by the chief priests and scribes: "He saved others... but he can't save himself. Let the Christ, the king of Israel, come down from the cross. Then we'll see and believe" (15:31-32).

Strong irony, rooted deeply within the theology of Mark's Gospel, is at work here.[13] The words of the passersby invert Jesus' own teaching. On the road to Jerusalem Jesus himself had rebuked Peter and spoke of the necessity of "taking up their cross" in order to be his followers (8:31-32).[14] He goes on to declare, "All who want to save their lives will lose them. But all who lose their lives because of me and because of the good news will save them" (8:35). The word *save* used in the taunts of the mockers and found in these discipleship sayings is the Greek term *sōzein*. At several points in the gospel, Mark uses this term to describe the impact of Jesus' healing mission. The woman with the hemorrhage (5:23, 28) is "saved" by contact with Jesus' dynamic power; so, too, are the sick around the village of Gennesaret (6:56), as is Bartimaeus in being healed of his blindness (10:52). To be "saved" (*sōzein*) indicates that the impact of Jesus' healings and exorcisms are not limited to physical transformation but touch the entire being of those in need. Thus it is profoundly true that the Jesus portrayed by Mark "loses" his life in selfless service (*diakonia*) and thereby "saves" others.

Likewise, the religious leaders mock Jesus for saving others but not being able to save himself (15:31)—unwittingly expressing the very heart of Jesus' own God-given messianic mission to not serve himself but to serve others (10:45). They think they are deriding Jesus in addressing him as "the Christ, the king of Israel" (15:32) when in fact the reader of the gospel has known from the beginning of the narrative that, in fact, Jesus is the true Messiah and king, one who exercises his power not in oppressing others as the rulers of the earth do but in humble service (10:42-45).[15] They propose that Jesus

---

12. See below, p. 39.

13. On the role of irony as a literary device in Greco-Roman literature, see Duke, *Irony in the Fourth Gospel*. Although Duke focuses on its use in John's Gospel, irony is at work in all four gospels and with particular force in the Passion Narratives.

14. See in ch. 6, "The Cross and Discipleship," pp. 119–20.

15. The mock homage given to Jesus as "king" in the Passion Narrative expresses the same kind of

save himself by coming down from the cross (15:32) when in the perspective of the gospel the cross of Jesus is the final expression of Jesus' mission to overcome evil and death.

And finally, the leaders propose that if Jesus separates himself from the cross, then they would "see and believe." Separating Jesus from his cross was, in effect, the proposal of Peter immediately after his confession at Caesarea Philippi (see 8:32-33)—earning a strong rebuke by Jesus himself: "Get behind me, Satan. You are not thinking God's thoughts but human thoughts" (8:33). To "see" Jesus without the cross, as the religious leaders propose, is, in the view of Mark's Gospel, to profoundly misunderstand who Jesus truly is.

The climax of Mark's Passion Narrative comes with the moment of Jesus' death (15:33-41). The final words of Jesus are a quotation from Psalm 22: "My God, my God why have you left me?" (15:34). As noted in chapter 2, this great lament psalm, with its movement from the anguish of lament to the triumphant experience of God's vindication, may well have been formative of the passion story before Mark's composition of his narrative.[16] But at this stage in the passion drama, the words of the psalm express Jesus' extreme distress and will feed into the somber tone of Mark's portrayal. In the Gethsemane account, Jesus had told his disciples that "I am very sad. It's as if I'm dying" (14:34), an anticipation of the distress that overwhelms Jesus at the moment of his death. Mark portrays a Jesus who gives his life for the many completely and without restraint. Even in these final moments, the bystanders continue to mock Jesus. One appears to distort his anguished prayer— "*Eloi, eloi*"—the Aramaic words reported by Mark for the beginning of Psalm 22, "My God, my God."[17] Some of the bystanders claim "Look! He's calling Elijah!" (15:35), and when someone goes to get a sponge soaked in "sour wine" for Jesus (possibly an allusion to Ps 68:22), the same bystanders repeat the line of mockery used by the religious leaders: "Let's see if Elijah will come to take him down" (15:36). Right to the bitter end, the opponents of Jesus continue to gravely misunderstand and distort Jesus' identity and mission by trying to separate him from the cross.[18]

---

irony on Mark's part. While the soldiers mock Jesus with a crown of thorns, a reed for scepter, and offer homage in jest, the reader knows the true identify of Jesus and these symbols of imperial power are themselves being revealed as empty. On the importance of the motif of kingship in Mark's Passion Narrative, see Matera, *The Kingship of Jesus*.

16. See pp. 23–28.

17. Mark has previously inserted Hebrew or Aramaic phrases, perhaps to give a certain archaic feel to the text; see Mark 5:41; 7:11, 34; 11:9, 10; 14:36; 15:22. On this see R. Brown, *The Death of the Messiah*, 1051–53.

18. Elijah is viewed as a kind of patron saint of hopeless cases; see R. Brown, *The Death of the Messiah*, 1062–63.

The actual moment of Jesus' death is described by Mark's Gospel in stark terms: "Jesus let out a loud cry and died" (15:37). The actual word for the instant of Jesus' death is *exepneusen*, meaning literally to "breathe out" or "expire." The death of Jesus is a total giving of life—his *pneuma* or "life breath" totally expended. The final cry of Jesus—literally, emitting a "loud sound" or "cry" (*phōnēn megalēn*)—has been interpreted in a variety of ways. For some it is simply a sign of Jesus' extreme anguish at the moment of his death. Others, noting that a similar phrase is found in some of the exorcism stories, view it as a sign of Jesus' own final confrontation with the power of death, or as a cry of victory as God's champion is about to triumph over the forces of evil.[19] While these wider symbolic interpretations may have merit, at the most fundamental level the final anguished cry of Jesus and the unadorned description of his final breath give to Mark's account a sobriety and completeness: as he promised, Jesus gives his life for the many.

Two dramatic events follow immediately upon the death of Jesus. First of all, "the curtain of the sanctuary was torn in two from top to bottom" (15:38). What does Mark's account wish to imply by noting this portent at the moment of Jesus' death? For some interpreters the tearing of the temple veil represents God's judgment on the temple, amplifying the motif of Jesus' prophetic action of the purification of the temple in 11:15-19.[20] The physical temple adorned and expanded by Herod the Great in Jerusalem would ultimately be destroyed and replaced by a "temple not made by hands"— the temple of which the Risen Jesus himself would be the cornerstone (see 12:10).

However, the symbolism of the tearing of the temple veil may also have a positive meaning, forming a kind of bracket or "inclusion" with the beginning of Jesus' ministry when the heavens split open and the power of the Spirit descends on Jesus at the moment of his baptism (1:10). The verb *schizomenos* is used in both instances. In some Jewish traditions the temple veil also symbolized the canopy of the heavens that separated the earthly realm from the divine.[21] Thus the impact of Jesus' death was to open a new way into the heavenly sanctuary—not unlike the theology of the Letter to the Hebrews that depicts Jesus as the "forerunner" who through his death and exaltation is the first to enter the heavenly sanctuary.[22]

---

19. See Danker, "The Demonic Secret in Mark."

20. See Donahue, *Are You the Christ?*, 103–38; Juel, *Messiah and Temple*, 117–210.

21. See the extended discussion in Collins, *Mark*, 759–64. She concludes that the tearing of the veil has a positive symbolic meaning, signifying the opening of the heavens or the barrier between humanity and God.

22. See below, pp. 107–10.

Mark's wording of the reaction of the centurion is also significant. Literally the text reads, "The centurion who stood facing Jesus, seeing how he expired, said, 'Truly this man was (the) Son of God'" (15:39 AT). The reaction of the centurion is triggered not by the tearing of the temple veil but precisely by seeing how Jesus died. Unlike the religious leaders who mock Jesus and challenge him to come down from the cross so that they can "see and believe," the centurion's reaction is in accord with Mark's theological perspective: in "seeing" that Jesus gives his life totally ("how he died"), the Roman officer acclaims Jesus as "truly the Son of God" (AT)! Irony is again at work: the first human being in the gospel narrative to recognize Jesus truly as the Son of God is a Roman centurion, who was one of those overseeing the crucifixion of Jesus! At the moment of his baptism and his being endowed with the Spirit (1:9-11), the voice of God had identified Jesus as "my Son, whom I dearly love." The same divine voice had identified the transfigured Jesus as "my Son, whom I dearly love" (9:7). The demonic spirits also recognized Jesus as God's son when recoiling from his power; they acknowledged him as "the holy one from God" (1:24) and as "the Son of the Most High God" (5:7). And now at the climax of the gospel narrative, it is a Roman soldier who is the first human being to fully confess Jesus as "God's Son"—a title that not only affirms the messianic identity of Jesus in the spirit of the enthronement psalm (Ps 110) but also expresses the full identity of Jesus as the one close to God and uniquely empowered with God's Spirit (Mark 1:9-11), one whose word is to be listened to intently (9:7).[23] The manner and purpose of Jesus' death reveals to the centurion, the first human witness, the divine power that is embodied in Jesus and gives saving power to his cross.

Signs of the Resurrection: The Empty Tomb

Mark's account of the discovery of the empty tomb of Jesus provides the final essential element in his proclamation of the saving power of the cross. The women who witness the death of Jesus "from a distance" (15:40) will become the key link between the crucifixion and the empty tomb. Mark describes them in terms that reflect their status as authentic disciples: they had "followed" Jesus in Galilee (the term *akolouthein*, "to follow," is virtually a technical term for discipleship), "served him" (AT; *diēkonoun*—the verb used to describe Jesus' own ministry of service), and "had come to Jerusalem with him"—participating in his fateful journey to the cross (15:41).

Along with the women, the account mentions Joseph of Arimathea, "a

23. On the meaning of the "Son of God" title in Mark's theology, see Senior, *The Passion of Jesus in the Gospel of Mark*, 94–97, 129–31.

prominent council member who also eagerly anticipated the coming of God's kingdom" (15:43)—also an indication of someone on the way to becoming a disciple of Jesus, reminiscent of the respectful scribe whom Jesus declared to be not far from the kingdom of God (12:34). Joseph acquires the dead body of Jesus from Pilate and sees to his burial in a rock-hewn tomb (15:46).

Mark's account does not include resurrection appearances; the announcement of the resurrection comes through the encounter of the women disciples with a heavenly messenger at the tomb.[24] The three women, who had witnessed Jesus' crucifixion, come on the day after the Sabbath to anoint his body and discover that the stone that had sealed the entrance was rolled back. When they enter the tomb they encounter to their amazement "a young man in a white robe" (16:5). This heavenly messenger proclaims the astounding message: "Don't be alarmed! You are looking for Jesus of Nazareth, who was crucified. He has been raised. He isn't here. Look, here's the place where they laid him" (16:6). The contrast is stark: the Jesus who was crucified has now been raised from the dead! The power of death had been broken; precisely what Jesus had declared through his passion predictions on the journey from Galilee to Jerusalem and at the Last Passover. The Jesus who had lost his life had saved it.

Jesus' victory over death now transforms the community of the disciples, who in the face of death, had abandoned Jesus and fled in fear. The heavenly messenger commands the women to "go, tell his disciples, especially Peter, that he is going ahead of you into Galilee. You will see him there, just as he told you" (16:7). Jesus had told them of this reassembly in Galilee at the Passover meal at the very moment he had also predicted their failure and dispersal: "Jesus said to them, 'You will all falter in your faithfulness to me. It is written, *I will hit the shepherd, and the sheep will go off in all directions.* But after I'm raised up, I will go before you to Galilee'" (14:27-28). Both the prediction of the disciples' failure and the promise of their reconciliation would be true. Thus in Mark's account, resurrection results in reconciliation and renewal of the mission of exorcism and healing that Jesus himself had entrusted to the disciples (see 6:13).

The women, thunderstruck by their encounter at the empty tomb, leave with "fear and ecstasy" (AT, *tromos kai ekstasis*) and set out on their mission without speaking (16:8). Some have suggested that the reference to the women's silence is terminal—that they do not report what they have experienced to the disciples and consequently the gospel story ends on another note of

---

24. Virtually all modern commentators accept that 16:1-8 was the original ending of Mark's Gospel. See the discussion in Collins, *Mark*, 797–801.

failure.[25] Yet this seems preposterous in the context of the gospel as a whole. The word of Jesus does not fail—and he had predicted that he would go ahead of the disciples to Galilee after he had been raised, despite their failure (14:27). The women's reaction of awe and silence fits into the biblical mode of reaction to a theophany, which the women had indeed encountered.

Thus the efforts of the power of death not only to destroy Jesus, the Son of God, but also to destroy his mission of transforming healing and liberation were radically thwarted. Through his cross and his victory over death, Jesus the Messiah and Son of God had made the cross both a sign and means of salvation.

The Gospel of Matthew

Matthew's proclamation of the saving power of Jesus' death on the cross has great similarity to that of Mark's Gospel but there are aspects unique to Matthew. Interpreters of Matthew's Gospel have long noted its profoundly Jewish character.[26] The evangelist is likely to have been a Jewish Christian, and the relationship of his community's faith in Jesus as the Messiah and Son of God to his Jewish heritage is a consuming interest. This Jewish tone of Matthew's Gospel also influences his portrayal of the death of Jesus and its significance.

The Mission of Jesus and Its Connection to His Crucifixion

Like Mark, Matthew clearly connects the mission of Jesus to its ultimate outcome in his death on the cross. Even in the opening scenes of Matthew's narrative, deadly hostility to Jesus breaks out in the attempt of Herod to eradicate the perceived threat of "the newborn king of the Jews" (2:2). The threat is averted only through the intervention of "an angel from the Lord" who instructs Joseph to flee with the child and his mother into Egypt (2:13-15). When the family is called out of Egypt (evoking the exodus of Israel itself), they are unable to return to Bethlehem because of the cruelty of Herod's son Archelaus, who was now ruling in Judea; once again divine intervention directs Joseph and his family to flee to Nazareth (2:19-23).

Hostility toward Jesus reemerges in his public mission after a series of his

---

25. See Donahue and Harrington, *The Gospel of Mark*, 460–61, who suggest that Mark says, in effect, that the only character worth imitating in the gospel is Jesus himself; his earliest followers, no matter what their merits, "are not as worthy of their imitation as Jesus is" (461).

26. See Senior, *The Gospel of Matthew at the Crossroads of Early Christianity*, 3–23, which surveys recent literature on this issue.

healings and exorcisms, particularly from Matthew 11 on. Jesus confronts his opponents in 11:16-19, noting that they had rejected John the Baptist, declaring the ascetical desert prophet to be possessed by a demon, while also rejecting Jesus, "a glutton and a drunk," as "a friend of tax collectors and sinners." This deadly hostility is reinforced in a series of conflict stories that Matthew absorbs from Mark (see Matt 12:1-14), concluding with the notice that "the Pharisees went out and met in order to find a way to destroy Jesus" (12:14).

In the course of his Gospel, Matthew also adopts Mark's pattern of the threefold passion predictions that punctuate the journey to Jerusalem (see Matt 16:21; 17:22-23; 20:17-19). As in the key text of Mark 10:45, so in Matthew 20:28 the evangelist affirms that the death of Jesus is equivalent to a profound act of "service" (*diakonia*), the giving of his life in ransom for the many—linking the healing and teaching ministry of Jesus and the opposition it arouses to his death on the cross. Also as in Mark, the hostility to Jesus mounts in intensity throughout the narrative and comes to its climax when Jesus enters Jerusalem and performs his prophetic action in the temple. The bitter discourse of Matthew 23—unique to Matthew's account—indicts the leaders for their hypocrisy and abuse of their office. A series of sharp confrontations with the religious leaders in and around the temple area concludes with Jesus' parable of the wicked tenants. The tenants were entrusted with the care of the vineyard but ultimately abuse and kill the messengers sent by the landowner and finally reject and even murder the son of the landowner, bringing down on them the wrath of the owner (21:41). The narrative leaves no doubt that this parable is a thinly veiled allegory about the death of Jesus himself; the quotation of Psalm 118 about the stone rejected by the builder becoming the cornerstone affirms Jesus' ultimate triumph over rejection and death (see 21:42-44). Matthew notes that the religious leaders realize that the parable is meant for them and are determined to find an opportunity to arrest Jesus, an opportunity that comes at the very beginning of the Passion Narrative in the person of Judas, who offers to betray Jesus (see 21:45-46; 26:3-4, 14-16).

One characteristic note in Matthew's portrayal of the ministry of Jesus is his emphasis on the obedience of Jesus to his Father's will—a strong motif of Matthew's Gospel as a whole. The tone is set in the temptation narrative that prefaces Jesus' public ministry. The evangelist portrays Jesus as rejecting the attempts of Satan to turn him aside from his God-given mission. Satan's lure is rejected by Jesus' repeated statements of dedication to God's will (see Matt 4:1-11).[27] The first words of the Matthean Jesus at his encounter with

---

27. Matthew's temptation scene is similar to Luke's version (4:1-13), although Luke's sequence is

John the Baptist at the Jordan—"this is necessary to fulfill all righteousness" (3:15)—affirm responsiveness to God's will as the leitmotif of Jesus' entire mission. Later, in a passage also characteristic of Matthew, Jesus acclaims his unique relationship with the Father: "I praise you, Father, Lord of heaven and earth, because you've hidden these things from the wise and intelligent and have shown them to babies. Indeed, Father, this brings you happiness. My Father has handed all things over to me. No one knows the Son except the Father. And nobody knows the Father except the Son and anyone to whom the Son wants to reveal him" (Matt 11:25-27; see also Luke 10:21-22).

Obedience to the will of the Father is also a recurring theme of Jesus' teaching in Matthew's Gospel. In the Lord's Prayer, the disciples are instructed to ask of the Father that "Your will be done, on earth as it is in heaven" (6:10 AT; the literal translation of a prayer that will be repeated by Jesus in his anguished prayer in Gethsemane: see Matt 26:42). In the Sermon on the Mount they are also urged to "desire first and foremost God's kingdom and God's righteousness" (6:33). Those who do "the will of my Father who is in heaven" belong to the family of Jesus (see 12:50). The opponents of Jesus, on the other hand, are characterized as those who "break the command of God" for the sake of their own traditions (15:3).

This sense of Jesus' intimacy with his Father and his devotion to doing God's will reemerge in the Passion Narrative of Matthew, where the issue of Jesus' trust in God and his obedience to the point of death is a hallmark of Matthew's theology of the cross.

Matthew 26:26-29: The Final Passover: For the Forgiveness of Sins

In the Passion Narrative (Matt 26–27), Matthew follows the account of Mark very closely, but there are a few changes that stand out, changes that add nuance to Matthew's theology of the cross.[28] As in Mark, this scene not only anticipates the Christian Eucharist but also within the context of the Passion Narrative serves as a final passion prediction, enabling Jesus himself, as it were, to interpret the meaning of the death he is about to experience. The bread broken is his body that will be broken on the anvil of the cross but will become life giving for the disciples of Jesus (26:26; cf. Mark 14:22).[29]

different, with the encounter at the temple coming as the finale, reflecting Luke's focus on Jerusalem and its temple. Both Matthew and Luke seem to draw on a common source here, named by scholars as Q (from the German word for "source," *Quelle*). This source, evidence for which is found only on the basis of common materials shared by Matthew and Luke, was apparently an early collection of mainly sayings and parables of Jesus.

28. See Senior, *The Passion Narrative according to Matthew*, which tracks this comparison in detail.

29. The slight differences that separate Matthew from Mark in Jesus' words over the bread are mainly

Matthew makes some significant changes in Jesus' words over the cup.[30] The cup of "my blood of the covenant" is "poured out for the many so that their sins may be forgiven" (26:28; cf. Mark 14:24, "This is my blood of the covenant, which is poured out for many"). As in Mark, the words of Jesus over the cup allude to the covenant renewal found in Exodus 24. The sprinkling of blood of the oxen on the altar and on the people signifies the life-giving bond of the covenant that is forged between Yahweh and Yahweh's people. Jesus' death is interpreted as a renewal of that covenant, expressing as it does the fierce love of the Father for the people, which drives the healing and reconciling mission of Jesus.

Matthew makes a minor change in the phrase "for the many"; in Mark the preposition is *hyper* ("for"); in Matthew it reads *peri* ("for"). Although the meaning of the two Greek words is virtually identical, the word *peri* is used in the Septuagint (Greek) version of Isaiah 53:4 (AT) where the Servant is described as carrying sickness "for us" (*peri*) and bearing suffering "for us" (*peri*). While neither Mark nor Matthew seem to emphasize the role of Jesus as the Suffering Servant, in this instance Matthew's text may draw more attention to the allusion through its choice of preposition.[31] We should also note that Matthew had interpreted the healing ministry of Jesus with a "fulfillment" quotation drawn precisely from Isaiah 53:4: "*He is the one who took our illnesses and carried away our diseases*" (Matt 8:17). Thus Jesus is the Servant in his acts of healing and liberation, which now come to final expression in his death for others.

Even more significant is Matthew's addition of the phrase "so that their sins maybe forgiven" to the words over the cup (Matt 26:28). The mission of Jesus to forgive sins was signaled at the very beginning of the Gospel. Along with the name *Emmanuel* ("God-with-us") given to the infant Christ, he is also to be named "Jesus, because he will save his people from their sins" (Matt 1:21). In the course of his pubic ministry, Matthew attributes the power to forgive sins to Jesus alone. In Mark's Gospel, the message of John is described as "calling for people to be baptized to show that they were changing their hearts and lives and wanted God to forgive their sins"; Matthew omits the reference to forgiveness of sins in his parallel verse (cf. Mark 1:4 and Matt 3:2). The "saving of his people from their sins" is particularly carried out in the

---

stylistic; he uses the word "disciples" instead of the pronoun "them" and adds the explicit command "eat," which is only implied in Mark—thereby balancing it with the command to "drink" in Matthew 26:27.

30. Some of Matthew's changes are again stylistic: e.g., the typical use of direct address ("Drink of it, all of you" compared to Mark's indirect, "and they all drank of it"); the addition of "for" (*gar*) making explicit the link implied in Mark's version.

31. See earlier, pp. 34–36.

healing mission of the Messiah Jesus who liberates human beings from the grip of sin and death (see Matt 8:17). Jesus forgives the sins of the paralyzed man brought to Jesus by his friends and, when challenged by his opponents, declares, "Which is easier—to say, 'Your sins are forgiven,' or to say, 'Get up and walk'? But so you will know that the Human One [literally "the Son of Man"] has authority on the earth to forgive sins—he said to the man who was paralyzed—'Get up, take your cot, and go home'" (Matt 9:5-6).

Therefore it is not surprising that in his words over the cup—Jesus' final interpretation of the meaning of his impending death—he sees his death as the culmination of a life of service and a means of forgiveness and reconciliation.

The Death of Jesus as a Consummate Act of Fidelity and Trust

As already noted, the Jewish tonalities of Matthew's portrayal of Jesus result in an emphasis on his obedience to the will of God. This motif carries over into the Passion Narrative of Matthew and becomes an integral part of his theology of the cross. It is through his unbreakable trust in God that Jesus turns back the assault of evil and death and is lifted up to new life through resurrection from the dead.[32]

The motif of Jesus' obedience to the will of God breaks into the open in Matthew's version of the Gethsemane scene (see 26:36-46).[33] Matthew's version of this scene has two major differences from his source Mark (see Mark 14:32-42). The threefold marking of Jesus' return to his sleeping disciples in Mark (14:37, 40, 41) becomes in Matthew's version Jesus' threefold return to his earnest prayer (26:42, 44). And the content of Jesus' prayer in Matthew's version is also significant. Matthew shares with Mark the dramatic prayer of Jesus that the "cup"—a clear reference to his impending death—might "be taken away." As in Mark's account, Jesus had spoken of his death as drinking "the cup that I'm about to drink" in his encounter with the sons of Zebedee (see Matt 20:22; parallel Mark 10:38).[34] Yet the decisive end of the prayer is Jesus' affirmation of his fidelity to God's will even in the face of death: "Father... not what I want but what you want" (Matt 26:39; similarly Mark 14:36). Matthew reinforces this fidelity of Jesus in the words of the second

---

32. Obviously Matthew's Gospel also presents this as an example for authentic discipleship; see below, pp. 47–50.

33. On the overall scene and its presentation in the four gospels and Hebrews, see R. Brown, *The Death of the Messiah*, 191–234.

34. The metaphor of the "cup" has several possible layers of meaning, but the dominant meaning in this context is the reference to Jesus' death. Matthew emphasizes this metaphor in his Gethsemane account, dropping Mark's other metaphor of "the hour" (or "time," CEB; see Mark 14:35).

prayer, a prayer not stated in Mark's version: "My Father, if it's not possible that this cup be taken away unless I drink it, then let it be what you want" (26:42).

In the second prayer there is a subtle movement towards the inevitability of Jesus' death ("if it's not possible...") and significantly the words of Jesus repeat a key petition of the Lord's prayer he had taught his disciples in the Sermon on the Mount: "Your will be done" (AT; see Matt 6:10). The Matthean Jesus faces death with integrity, prayerful before the "test," as he had instructed his disciples to be, and bending to God's will no matter how baffling it might seem (see 6:13; 25:13; 26:38). In the arrest scene that immediately follows, the Matthean Jesus reaffirms this sense of obedience when he deflects the use of the sword by one of his disciples by stating, "Do you think that I'm not able to ask my Father and he will send to me more than twelve battle groups of angels right away? But if I did that, how would the scriptures be fulfilled that say this must happen?" (26:53-54).

The Death of Jesus

Matthew's emphasis on the fidelity of Jesus to God's will and his trust in God's faithfulness come into full view at the crucifixion scene (27:38-56), where he intensifies the role of the lament psalm (Ps 22) as a backdrop for Jesus' death and vindication.[35] As in Mark, the scene begins with the passersby and the religious leaders mocking Jesus as he hangs on the cross. Their first taunt is Jesus' alleged threat against the temple that had been brought up by false witnesses at the hearing before the Sanhedrin (see 26:60-61).[36] Matthew interjects the phrase "If you are God's Son," recalling the taunting words of Satan in the desert test (see 4:3, 6). The mocking proposal of Jesus' tormentors is that he "come down from the cross" and "save himself"—ironic twists on Jesus' own teaching about the necessity of embracing the cross and saving one's life by losing it (see 16:24-25).[37] Matthew's focus, however, extends again to the issue of trust through his addition of verse 43: "He trusts in God, so let God deliver him now, if he wants to. He said, 'I'm God's Son.'" This is a direct quote from Psalm 22:8 and Wisdom 2:18. The mockers put to the test the trust the Just One places in God: *Is God faithful?* these words dare to ask.

Once again echoing his source Mark, Matthew makes the first words of

---

35. On the role of Psalm 22 as a lament psalm, see earlier, pp. 23–28.

36. Matthew introduces a subtle change in the charge at the trial; the witness says that Jesus claimed "I can destroy God's temple" (26:61); compare to Mark's version: "I will destroy this temple, constructed by humans" (14:58)—a change that may reflect Matthew's more reverential attitude towards the Jerusalem temple.

37. As in Mark, see previously, pp. 36–39.

Psalm 22 the last words that the Crucified Jesus speaks: "My God, my God, why have you left me?" (27:46). Matthew makes some subtle changes that highlight both the use of Psalm 22 and his emphasis on the obedience of Jesus. He states, "Again Jesus cried out with a loud shout" (27:50). The Greek verb for "cry out" is different from Mark's phrase (*apheis phōnēn megalēn*, i.e., "letting out a loud cry" [Mark 15:37]); Matthew uses the simple verb *kraxas* ("to cry out"), the same verb used several times in Psalm 22 to describe the anguished lament of the psalmist (Ps 22:2, 5, 24). Together with the adverb "again" (*palin*), Matthew's changes clearly imply that at the very moment of his death Jesus once more prays the words of Psalm 22.

Additionally, Matthew also makes a small but significant change in his description of Jesus' last breath. Where Mark, portraying Jesus' death as a total giving of his life, uses the stark word *exepneusen* (literally, "expires"), Matthew, introducing a note of intent or deliberation, uses the phrase *aphēken to pneuma* (literally "yielded" or "handed over" the spirit). The creation account of Genesis 2:7 describes God "breathing" (*enephysēsen*) into the face of the human to create human life, animating the bag of clay that now becomes a human being. As Jewish tradition reflected, giving back to God the *pneuma* or life breath that belongs to God in the first place is the proper and reverential act of the mortal before the mystery of death. In the dramatic description of death gripping the village, the author of Qohelet (Ecclesiastes) portrays the death of the human as "the dust returns to the earth as it was, and the breath [*pneuma*] returns to God who gave it" (Eccl 12:7 LXX).[38] Thus Matthew appears to portray Jesus' final moment of life as an act of trust, even in the midst of anguish; he prays in lament but also entrusts his very being to God his Father and the author and source of all life.[39]

Signs of Resurrection

More explicitly and dramatically than any of the other gospels, Matthew affirms the vindication of Jesus' fidelity and trust in the astounding events that break out at the very moment of Jesus' death. In one extended sentence, the evangelist describes the tearing of the temple veil, an earthquake, the splitting open of the rocks, the opening of the tombs, the liberation of "bodies of many holy people," their entrance into the "holy city" and their appearances

---

38. Davies and Allison, *Matthew*, refers also to the death of Rachel in Gen 35:18, who also yields her life-breath as she dies.

39. As Hagner notes, Matthew's portrayal of Jesus' final moment stands between the abject description of Mark and the clearer deliberation of Luke ("Into your hands I entrust my life," 23:46) and John ("It is completed," 19:30); see Hagner, *Matthew 14–28*, 845.

to many (27:52-53). These portents are clearly apocalyptic signs, indicating that the final day of the Lord was breaking into history. Matthew most likely draws this description from Ezekiel's famous vision of the dry bones (Ezek 37:1-14), where the "dry bones" of Israel, laying scattered and lifeless in exile on the desert floor, are infused with God's spirit and become a living people who are able to reassemble and return to their own land.[40]

Matthew clearly anticipates the resurrection here, even causing himself some chronological difficulties. Since the account of the empty tomb and Jesus' own resurrection appearances (see 28:9-10, 16-20) are still to come, the evangelist has to note that the appearances of those who are raised from the dead and come out of their tombs, make their appearances only "after Jesus' resurrection" (27:53)! Nevertheless, Matthew's theological point is made: the anguished yet trusting prayer of Jesus the Son of God is heard by his Father and his trust is resoundingly vindicated in the outbreak of new life.

These events prompt the confession of the centurion—now joined in Matthew's version by "those with him" (27:54). Witnessing God's extraordinary vindication of Jesus' trust, they proclaim, "This was certainly God's Son" (27:54). The taunt of Satan—"if you are the Son of God"—which is repeated by the religious leaders at the moment of the crucifixion, is definitely answered! Matthew's key christological title for Jesus is confirmed: Jesus the Son of God, that is, the royal Davidic Messiah and the one who experiences unique intimacy with his Father (11:25-27), is most visibly so at the moment of his giving of life for the world. The power of evil and death, already under assault through Jesus' ministry of healing and teaching, is definitively broken. The Son of Man's authority to forgive sins now lifts the dead from their graves and forges a renewed people.

For Matthew's Gospel the death and resurrection of Jesus is the turning point in history; the old world under the sway of death is passing away and the new world of abundant life begins to break out. This is further signaled with the discovery of the empty tomb. Matthew adds dramatic apocalyptic coloring to this account; there is another earthquake and an "angel from the Lord" descends from heaven and rolls back the stone from the tomb (28:2). The appearance of this heavenly messenger causes the guards, futilely set at the tomb at the request of Jesus' opponents, to tremble in fear and become "like dead men" (28:2-4). And not only is it the angel who interprets the meaning of the empty tomb to the women witnesses ("He isn't here, because

---

40. This text is given a messianic interpretation in the famous Ezekiel panel of the Dura-Europos synagogue. It is the Messiah who breathes God's spirit on the dry bones, and they assemble and march into Jerusalem. See also the possible influence of Dan 12:2, which refers to the dead awakening to new life.

he's been raised from the dead, just as he said" [28:6]), but also the Risen Jesus himself appears to the women as they leave the tomb and reinforces their mission to announce the resurrection to "my brothers" in Galilee where "they will see me" (28:9-10).[41]

The dramatic concluding scene of Matthew's Gospel (28:16-20) deserves attention in its own right for its theology of mission and its summation of the overall theology of Matthew's Gospel. For our purposes, however, we can note that this scene is the final outcome of the death and resurrection of Jesus as presented by Matthew's Gospel. The mission of Jesus seemingly cut short by his crucifixion and death is now fully vindicated and reaches its ultimate expression in this final resurrection appearance of Matthew's Gospel. Not only are the disciples who failed Jesus rehabilitated—continuing the note of reconciliation that plays a role in all of the gospel resurrection appearance accounts—but also the charge given them by the Risen Christ now takes them beyond Israel to "all nations." In Matthew's view of history, the death and resurrection of Jesus becomes the crucial turning point, as the apocalyptic signs that erupt at the moment of his death illustrate. The mission of the Messiah Jesus restricted to Israel during his earthly ministry prior to his death and resurrection (see 10:5 and 15:24) now opens to the world. Just as the teaching of Jesus did not "do away with the Law and the Prophets" but "fulfill them" (5:17), so the mission to the nations brings to its ultimate expression God's intention to save all nations, through the instrumentality of Jesus and the community formed in his name. The mission to the Gentiles does not replace or supersede the mission to Israel but is its flowering. The cross as the culmination of Jesus' mission of healing and teaching directed to Israel is, through his fidelity to God's will and the power of the resurrection, now bursting into new life as an embrace of the whole world.[42]

The Gospel of Luke

Like his two Synoptic counterparts, Luke's Gospel portrays the crucifixion of Jesus as both a saving event and a turning point in history. Some interpreters of Luke have claimed that the redemptive significance of the cross

---

41. In the Last Supper account, when predicting his death and resurrection in terms of the renewed Passover meal, Matthew adds to Mark's version the promise that Jesus would drink the fruit of the vine "with you in my Father's kingdom" (26:29), a note of intimacy with the disciples also reflected here in the words of Jesus to the women.

42. On this view of the mission to the nations in Matthew's theology, see especially Konradt, *Israel, Kirche und die Völker im Matthäusevangelium*; see also Cuvillier, "La construction narrative de la mission dans le premier évangile," in Senior, *The Gospel of Matthew at the Crossroads of Early Christianity*, 159–75.

is played down in this gospel compared to the others. For example, Luke omits the reference to Jesus' death as a "ransom for the many" found in the key text of Mark 10:45 and Matthew 20:28 (AT).[43] Luke seems to present the death of Jesus as merely a step in the final sequence of his messianic mission: "Wasn't it necessary for the Christ to suffer these things and then enter into his glory?" as the Risen Jesus explains to his disciples on the road to Emmaus (see Luke 24:26). Yet while Luke may not explicitly utilize imagery drawn from the portrait of the Suffering Servant as Matthew and Mark do, he still portrays the death of Jesus itself as having saving significance.

Jesus: The Spirit-Filled Prophet and Martyr

One of the dominant and characteristic images in Luke's portrayal of Jesus is his identity as a prophet, one who like the prophets of Israel suffered rejection and persecution in the course of his God-given mission to Israel.[44] Luke sets the stage for this in the inaugural scene of Jesus' public ministry in his hometown synagogue of Nazareth, a scene unique to Luke's Gospel (see 4:16-30) and one that serves as an overture to the gospel as a whole. Jesus deliberately selects the reading from Isaiah 61:

The LORD God's spirit is upon me,
> because the LORD has anointed me.
He has sent me
> to bring good news to the poor,
> to bind up the brokenhearted,
> to proclaim release for captives,
> > and liberation for prisoners,
> to proclaim the year of the LORD's favor.[45]

Several key motifs that will characterize Jesus' mission in Luke are already anticipated in this inaugural scene. First of all, Luke places particular emphasis on Jesus' endowment with the Spirit as signaled in his quotation of Isaiah 61 as the keynote of his ministry ("Today, this scripture has been fulfilled

---

43. On this discussion, see Green, "'He Saved Others; Let Him Save Himself'" in Carroll and Green, *The Death of Jesus in Early Christianity*, 60–81; Green, "'Was It Not Necessary for the Messiah to Suffer These Things and Enter into His Glory?'" in Marshall, Rabens, and Bennema, *The Spirit and Christ in the New Testament and Christian Theology*; and Fitzmyer, *The Gospel according to Luke I–IX*, 22–23.

44. The classic text is that of Neh 9:26-31, "They killed your prophets who had warned them so that they might return to you" (v. 26).

45. The text as cited by Luke is an adaptation of Isa 61:1-2 found in both the Hebrew and Septuagint (Greek) versions.

just as you heard it," Luke 4:21). In both his Gospel and in the Acts of the Apostles, Luke identifies the Spirit as the driving force of Jesus' mission and of the post-Easter community that will be endowed with the Spirit through the mediation of the Risen and Glorified Christ.[46]

Second, Luke portrays the messianic mission of Jesus as bringing the power of God's justice to those in need: those who are poor, captive, blind, oppressed. The Galilean ministry of Jesus will be filled with illustrations of this mission, from the cleansing of the leper and the healing of the paralytic (5:12-26) to the raising of the widow of Nain's son (7:11-17) and the Sabbath healings of the woman bent double (13:10-17) and the man with dropsy (14:1-6). Parables unique to Luke also illustrate this dimension of Jesus' mission, several of which warn the rich not to neglect the poor.[47] This message of justice for those who are vulnerable and in need evokes the voice of the prophets of Israel who also challenged Israel for its lack of justice and the need to care for the widow, the sojourner, and the orphan. The crowds who witness Jesus' raising of the son of the widow from the dead at Nain exclaim, "A great prophet has appeared among us. . . . God has come to help his people" (7:16).

Third, Luke emphasizes the boundary-breaking character of Jesus' messianic mission. While his hometown audience of Nazareth might ask him to do there what they had heard of his deeds in Capernaum, Jesus provocatively recalls the mission of Elijah to Namaan the Syrian and that of Elisha to the widow of Zarephath in Sidon (Luke 4:24-27; see 1 Kgs 17:9 and 2 Kgs 5:14). Here we have a glimpse of the expansive horizon of Luke's Gospel and its follow-up in the Acts of the Apostles. God's salvation that breaks into the world with the advent of Jesus will surge out into the whole world.

The outcome of Jesus' inaugural proclamation is to trigger the hostility of his hometown audience. Just as the prophets of Israel were rejected and threatened with persecution and death, so the people of Nazareth rise up in indignation and attempt to hurl Jesus off the cliff at the edge of the town (4:29). Several times in Luke's Gospel, Jesus alludes to the fate of the prophets.[48] A most telling text in Luke is Jesus' retort to Herod Antipas when some Pharisees warn Jesus that the ruler was seeking to kill him:

> "Go, tell that fox, 'Look, I'm throwing out demons and healing people today and tomorrow, and on the third day I will complete my work. However, it's necessary for me to travel today, tomorrow, and the next day because it's impossible for a prophet to be killed outside of Jerusalem.'

---

46. On the role of the Spirit in Luke–Acts, see Johnson, *Prophetic Jesus, Prophetic Church*, esp. 52–71.

47. See Luke 12:13-21; 14:15-24; 16:19-31.

48. See, e.g., Luke 6:22-23; 11:47-50.

"Jerusalem, Jerusalem, you who kill the prophets and stone those who were sent to you! How often I have wanted to gather your people just as a hen gathers her chicks under her wings. But you didn't want that. Look, your house is abandoned. I tell you, you won't see me until the time comes when you say, *Blessings on the one who comes in the Lord's name*." (Luke 13:32-35)

Thus for Luke, Jesus is the Spirit-filled prophet who brings forgiveness and salvation to those in need, not only to those in Israel but also, as already illustrated in Jesus' boundary-breaking ministry, through the Spirit of God, to the ends of the earth. But, at the same time, this prophet—like the prophets of old—would face opposition and even death in the pursuit of his mission.

The Journey to God

The conclusion of the Nazareth scene also hints at another characteristic feature of Luke's Gospel, namely the journey of Jesus to Jerusalem. Although the townspeople attempt to kill Jesus by throwing him off a cliff, Jesus "passed through the crowd and went on his way" (4:30). Luke significantly expands this motif of Jesus' ministry as a "journey" to Jerusalem already found in Mark's Gospel and continued in Matthew as well; for Luke, the ultimate endpoint of the journey is Jesus' ascension to the right hand of God. Luke describes the time drawing near as the days of Jesus' "being taken up" (*analēmpseōs*; Luke 9:51), a reference therefore not only to his arrival in Jerusalem but also to the full span of events that Luke will narrate, namely the death, resurrection, and ascension of Jesus.[49] Thus for Luke the death of Jesus on the cross is a "necessity" ("the Messiah *had* to suffer. . ."), not as a grim stroke of fate but as the outcome of a prophetic and redemptive mission of healing, inclusion, and justice for the salvation of the world.

The Assault of Satan and the Power of Darkness

As already noted, Luke underscores the role of Satan as the ultimate source of opposition to Jesus.[50] At one profound level, Luke conceives of the death of Jesus as a final confrontation with the power of evil—a power he had already confronted in the healings and exorcisms of his ministry but was now coming to its final struggle on the cross. The forces arrayed against Jesus are, on one level, human actors—the religious leaders, Pilate, the soldiers, the

---

49. See also Luke 9:31 where during the transfiguration Moses and Elijah talk about Jesus' "departure" (literally, "his exodus") that would take place in Jerusalem.

50. See earlier, pp. 22–23.

crowds and the passersby—but on a deeper level the driving force that opposes Jesus as God's Holy One and as the Spirit-endowed liberator and Messiah is the very personification of evil. As Jesus declares to those who come to arrest him, led by Judas the betrayer, "But this is your time, when darkness rules" (22:53). As Luke's Gospel and the Acts of the Apostles will proclaim, the "power of darkness" will be broken through the death, resurrection, and exaltation of Jesus.

Luke 22:7-38: The Final Passover: "I am among you as one who serves."

Luke's account of the Last Supper differs significantly from that of Mark and Matthew, especially by adding discourse material at the conclusion of the meal. Luke also begins with a more emphatic focus on the Passover meal itself before turning to Jesus' words over the bread and cup. Jesus takes the initiative to prepare for the Passover meal by sending "Peter and John" into the city to make the arrangements (22:7-13; in Mark and Matthew, it is the disciples who approach Jesus about making the preparations). Jesus begins the meal with a poignant statement: "I have earnestly desired to eat this Passover with you before I suffer. I tell you, I won't eat it again until it is fulfilled in God's kingdom" (22:15-16). He goes on to take a cup, give thanks, and distribute it among his disciples, repeating his declaration—"I tell you that from now on I won't drink from the fruit of the vine until God's kingdom has come" (22:18).

Although the Passover festival had multiple meanings at different stages in Israel's history, its core significance was both retrospective—recalling God's great redemptive act in delivering Israel from slavery and bringing them to a land of promise—and prospective—longing for the final experience of redemption that would come in the final days ("Next year in Jerusalem!"). The words of Jesus at the beginning of Luke's Last Supper account resonate with both of these dimensions. Jesus celebrates God's act of redemption with his disciples, a ritual that in the setting of the Passion Narrative gives a new level of meaning to Jesus' own mission of liberation and healing. As Jesus celebrates the Passover he has in mind his approaching sufferings ("before I suffer"). At the same time, Jesus emphasizes the finality of this Passover, which will only be renewed when it is celebrated in the kingdom of God: "I tell you, I won't eat it until it is fulfilled in God's kingdom"; "I tell you that from now on I won't drink from the fruit of the vine until God's kingdom has come." Standing between these moments of the final Passover with his disciples and its triumphant renewal in the kingdom of God is the death and resurrection of Jesus, the great act of definitive liberation from evil and death that would usher in the kingdom of God.

Luke follows this initial focus on the Passover meal itself (with the drinking of the cup a key element) with the so-called institution account that is closer to the versions of Mark and Matthew (see Luke 22:19-31). Luke's version of Jesus' words also shares some similarity with Paul's account in 1 Corinthians 11:23-25; for example, he adds the phrase "which is for you" to Jesus' words over the bread, as well as the command, "Do this in remembrance of me" (Luke 22:19; cf. 1 Cor 11:24). Luke also rephrases Jesus' words over the cup: "This cup is the new covenant by my blood, which is poured out for *you*" (Luke 22:20, italics added; cf. Mark and Matthew, "for many" in Mark 14:24; Matt 26:28) and "is the new covenant by my blood" (Luke 22:20, as in 1 Cor 11:25; cf. Mark and Matthew, "my blood of the covenant"; Mark 14:24; Matt 26:28).

Luke's wording emphasizes that the breaking and giving of the bread is "given for you" and that the cup of wine to be shared among the disciples is wine poured out "for you." Just as the healings, exorcisms, and life-giving teaching of Jesus meant transformation and liberation for the sick and the poor he had encountered, so the death of Jesus—the body broken, the blood poured out—would be an ultimate act of life giving for his disciples.

Additionally, this definitive act of Jesus' mission would establish a "new covenant by his blood." In adding the term *new covenant*, Luke seems to also allude to the covenant renewal described in Jeremiah 31:31-34:

> The time is coming, declares the LORD, when I will make a new covenant with the people of Israel and Judah. It won't be like the covenant I made with their ancestors when I took them by the hand to lead them out of the land of Egypt. They broke that covenant with me even though I was their husband, declares the LORD. No, this is the covenant that I will make with the people of Israel after that time, declares the LORD. I will put my Instructions within them and engrave them on their hearts. I will be their God, and they will be my people. They will no longer need to teach each other to say, "Know the LORD!" because they will all know me, from the least of them to the greatest, declares the LORD; for I will forgive their wrongdoing and never again remember their sins.

The emphasis of this passage on renewal and forgiveness resonates well with the mission of Jesus as portrayed in Luke's Gospel. The final injunction of the Risen Christ to his disciples immediately before his ascension asks them to recall everything he had taught them about the scriptures ("that everything written about me in the Law from Moses, the Prophets, and the Psalms must be fulfilled"), to recall also that "the Christ will suffer and rise from the dead on the third day," and "and a change of heart and life for the forgiveness of sins must be preached in his name to all nations, beginning from Jerusalem" (Luke 24:44, 46-47). This is the ultimate meaning of Jesus' death and resurrection the disciples are asked to "remember" ("Do this in remembrance of me," 22:19)—a sacred obligation that would be carried out by the preaching and witness of the apostles in the Acts of the Apostles.

In Luke's account the Passover meal concludes with a final discourse of Jesus. In a remarkable scene the disciples begin a dispute about "which one of them should be regarded as the greatest," material that Mark had placed during the journey of Jesus and his disciples to Jerusalem (Luke 22:24; see Mark 9:33-37; especially 10:35-45). Luke's placing this dispute in the immediate context of Jesus' final meal with his disciples dramatically sharpens the contrast between Jesus' words and the behavior and attitude of his disciples. They argue about greatness while Jesus speaks about his giving of his life for them. Jesus responds by contrasting his own use of power "as one who serves" with that of "the kings of the Gentiles" who oppress their subjects.[51] Here again the ministry of Jesus is characterized as "service" (*diakonia*); as we noted Luke does not cite the words of Jesus about his "serving" (*diakonein*) as in the key text of Mark 10:45 (parallel Matt 20:28), but he does have the equivalent here at the Last Supper. In contrast to the abusive and oppressive exercise of authority by "the kings of the Gentiles," Jesus, the Davidic Messiah, exercises his power in giving life to others. The placement of this fundamental interpretation here at the Last Passover surely indicates that Luke sees the death of Jesus as his final act of service, in the manner of the Servant of Israel who gave his life in ransom for the many.

In the words that follow, Jesus commends his disciples for having stood by him "in my trials" (*peirasmois*) (22:28) and warns them of the assault of evil on them as well.[52]

Once again Luke portrays the death of Jesus as the definitive struggle with the forces of evil, the culmination of a struggle noted throughout his ministry.

Jesus: The Exemplary Prophet and Martyr

One clear dimension of Luke's Passion Narrative is his portrayal of Jesus as a courageous and exemplary prophetic model in the face of opposition and

---

51. Note that Luke uses the meal image here: "So which one is greater, the one who is seated at the table or the one who serves at the table? Isn't it the one who is seated at the table?" (22:27). Throughout his Gospel, Luke has emphasized the meal setting of so much of Jesus' mission, and that continues here; see Karris, *Luke*, esp. 47–78.

52. On the motif of perseverance in Luke, see S. Brown, *Apostasy and Perseverance*, esp. 53–81.

death. Thus on the Mount of Olives following the Passover meal he prays earnestly for the strength to face the test that awaits him (22:39-45). He rejects violence at the moment of his arrest, telling his disciples not to use the sword and healing the severed ear of the high priest's slave (22:51). He endures unjust accusations even though his innocence is affirmed by both Pilate (23:4, 13-17) and Herod Antipas (23:6-12). He is mocked as a false prophet but remains silent (22:63-65). His claim to be the Messiah and the Son of God is rejected by the council of religious leaders but he replies courageously (22:66-71). He consoles the people of Jerusalem who mourn for him, warning them of the days of travail that would befall them (23:27-31). He forgives those who crucify him (23:34),[53] and offers a promise of salvation to the good thief (23:39-43). He dies entrusting his spirit to his Father in the words of Psalm 31:6.

The Death of Jesus: "Truly this man was just." (Luke 23:47 AT)

Yet Luke understands the meaning of Jesus' death on the cross as more than a moral example for Christian life and as more than a necessary stage on the path to resurrection and exaltation. As in Mark and Matthew's accounts, the death of the Crucified Jesus is prefaced with mockery. In Luke's account the mockers challenge Jesus on his claim to be the "Christ sent from God, the chosen one" (23:35), echoing the challenge of the council at the "trial" of Jesus (see 22:67).[54] "He saved others. Let him save himself" (23:35). Here again irony is close to the surface of the passion account. At the inaugural scene of his mission, Jesus himself would announce his mission of salvation in the words of Isaiah 61: bringing good news to the poor, release to captives, recovery of sight to the blind, and freeing the oppressed (4:18-19). As he announces to Zacchaeus, "Today, salvation has come to this household, because he too is a son of Abraham. The Human One came to seek and to save the lost" (19:9-10). The leaders who mock Jesus challenge him in words that are twisted refrains from Jesus' own teaching. Jesus himself had instructed his disciples that "all who want to save their lives will lose them. But all who lose their lives because of me will save them" (9:24). Jesus, God's anointed, reveals his identity as Messiah precisely in giving his life for others.

The mockeries continue, now focusing on Jesus' claim to be "the king of

---

53.   Some early manuscripts omit this verse but it is present in other major Greek codices and early translations. For an extensive discussion, see R. Brown, *The Death of the Messiah*, 971–81, who concludes it is most probably authentic to Luke.

54.   Luke omits their claim about Jesus' threats against the temple, perhaps because of the positive role the temple plays in his Gospel and in Acts.

57

the Jews." Soldiers, presumably those who had crucified Jesus and then stood watch over the execution, offer Jesus "sour wine," while mocking him: "If you really are the king of the Jews, save yourself" (23:36-37). The inscription over the cross is also seen by Luke as part of the mockery: "This is the king of the Jews" (23:38) and one of the thieves crucified alongside Jesus also joins in: "Aren't you the Christ? Save yourself and us!" (23:39). A distinctive element of Luke's passion account is that the accusations against Jesus include charges of sedition. The religious leaders tell Pilate, "We have found this man misleading our people, opposing the payment of taxes to Caesar, and claiming that he is the Christ, a king" (23:2) and when Pilate resists they repeat the charge: "He agitates the people with his teaching throughout Judea—starting from Galilee all the way here" (23:5). The reader of Luke's Gospel knows that, in fact, Jesus *is* a king—the Son of David as announced by heavenly messengers in the infancy narrative (1:32-33; 2:10-12, 25-32) and demonstrated throughout the gospel by Jesus' power to heal and cast out evil. But, as Jesus had instructed his disciples at the final Passover, his kingship would not be exercised in the manner of the "kings of the Gentiles," who oppressed and dominated their subjects, but by serving and giving his life that others might live (22:24-27).

Luke introduces the actual moment of Jesus' death in dramatic fashion. The "darkness," already a feature in Mark's account, is now intensified—"the sun stopped shining" (23:45). Luke may be alluding to Joel 2:30-31, which describes the terror and chaos of the final days: "I will give signs in the heavens and on the earth—blood and fire and columns of smoke. The sun will be turned to darkness, and the moon to blood before the great and dreadful day of the LORD comes." The tearing of the temple veil that was a result of Jesus' death in Mark and Matthew in Luke's version takes place before Jesus dies. Because Luke views the temple in generally positive terms, the tearing of the veil as this moment may signify the final assault of the power of evil.[55] When the armed mob had come to arrest Jesus, he had challenged them: "Day after day I was with you in the temple, but you didn't arrest me. But this is your time, when darkness rules" (22:53). Now extreme darkness descends over Golgotha and the power of darkness assaults the very house of God and God's own Messiah.

Out of this darkness and chaos comes the final prayer of the dying Jesus: "Crying out in a loud voice, Jesus said, '*Father, into your hands I entrust my life*'" (literally, "my spirit," *to pneuma mou*; 23:46). In Luke's account Jesus cites the opening of Psalm 31, an eloquent prayer of both praise and anguish

---

55. See Senior, *The Passion of Jesus in the Gospel of Luke*, 138–43. R. Brown, *The Death of the Messiah*, 1102–6, interprets Luke's reference to the darkness and the tearing of the temple veil as a sign of God's wrath.

where the psalmist prays earnestly for deliverance in the midst of assault—"I take refuge in you, Lord. Please never let me be put to shame. Rescue me by your righteousness! Listen closely to me! Deliver me quickly; be a rock that protects me; be a strong fortress that saves me!"—and also one of intense trust in God—"I trust you, Lord! I affirm, 'You are my God'" (vv. 1-2, 14). The tone and content of the psalm fit well into the scene Luke portrays. Surrounded by mockery that puts in question his identity as God's Messiah and God's chosen one and in the midst of the fury of evil's final assault that darkens the sun's light and tears at the house of God, Jesus entrusts his spirit to his Father. Jesus who had "overflowed with joy from the Holy Spirit" and thanked his Father for the intimate love that surrounded him (10:21-22) now places his life in God's hands.

The Impact of Jesus' Death on the Cross

Luke affirms God's vindication of Jesus' trust and his Messianic mission in the events that immediately follow. The centurion who witnessed the final portents and Jesus' death—Luke refers to the "happenings" (AT; *to genomenon*)—praises God and declares, "It's really true: this man was righteous" (23:47) The term used for "righteous" or "just" is the Greek term *dikaios*, which can mean "innocent" as some notable translations prefer.[56] This would align the centurion's testimony with that of Pilate and Herod during the trial of Jesus, who both had insisted on Jesus' being innocent of the charges against him. The acclamation of the centurion at the moment of Jesus' death would serve what many interpreters see as an apologetic dimension to Luke's Gospel and to Acts: the evangelist has Roman authorities themselves declare Jesus innocent of the charges of sedition brought against him.[57] While this intent cannot be ruled out, the term *dikaios* has a much deeper resonance within the Bible and within Luke's Gospel. While Luke can use the term in a somewhat pejorative sense, referring to those who claim or arrogantly assume being "just" or "righteous" (see 5:32; 18:9; 20:20), in its positive use in the gospel, being "just" means someone who is "right with God" and lives a life of integrity such as Zechariah and Elizabeth, whom Luke describes as "both righteous before God, blameless in their observance of all the Lord's commandments and regulations" (1:6). Likewise Joseph of Arimathea, who would bury the Crucified Jesus, is described as "a good and righteous [*dikaios*]

---

56. Both the *New Revised Standard* and the *New American Bible* versions use "innocent."

57. But see the work of Rowe, *World Upside Down*, which illustrates how Luke, while affirming that Jesus and the apostles were not revolutionaries in the ordinary sense of the term, also intends to show how the Christian message is a profound challenge to the values and claims of the empire.

man" who although a member of the council "hadn't agreed to their plan and actions" (23:50-51). The testimony of the centurion, therefore, not only declares Jesus innocent of the crimes he had been accused of, but as he "praised God," the centurion even more importantly gives witness that Jesus was indeed someone who had trusted God and lived and died with integrity. Jesus the prophet-martyr died as he had lived—with complete trust and fidelity.

Luke describes the transforming impact of Jesus' death on other characters at the cross. In a note unique to Luke's account, the crowds who had witnessed Jesus' death also feel its impact. The death of Jesus the "just" one moves them to repentance. They return home "beating their chests" (23:48), recalling the attitude of the tax collector in Jesus' parable of the Pharisee and the tax collector (18:9-14).

Other witnesses are included in Luke's scene. The women "who had followed him from Galilee" (see 8:1-3) are standing at a distance, "observing these things" (23:49). Three of these women—Mary Magdalene, Joanna, and Mary "the mother of James"—will be the witnesses to the burial of Jesus and will be the ones to discover the empty tomb and the first to announce it to the apostles (23:55; 24:10).[58] To these Luke adds another enigmatic reference. Joining the women at the cross is "everyone who knew him" (23:49). Who are these unnamed witnesses? It is possible that this is Luke's tentative way of placing the apostles into the crucifixion account. Luke portrays the apostles as the key link between the mission of Jesus and the birth of the post-community. At the Last Passover Jesus prays for their perseverance (22:31). In contrast to Mark and Matthew, Luke's Gospel remains silent about the flight of the disciples at the moment of the arrest. And when Peter is in the midst of his denials, Jesus turns and looks at Peter, triggering his memory of Jesus' words to him and leading to Peter's tears of repentance (22:54-62). The reference to "everyone who knew him" at the cross might therefore be Luke's attempt to keep the disciples of Jesus from total abandonment of their master. They may be weak and battered by the experience of the passion and the test imposed by evil, but they are still present and have persevered because of Jesus' prayer for them.

The Empty Tomb and the Appearances of the Risen Christ

At the conclusion of the gospel narrative, Luke provides a series of events that indeed confirm God's vindication of Jesus and the efficacy of his life and death. The first is the discovery of the empty tomb (24:1-12). The women who had witnessed the crucifixion of Jesus go to the tomb after the Sab-

---

58. Luke observes that the women's testimony was judged "nonsense" and not believed by the apostles (24:11)!

bath to anoint the body of Jesus, and at the now-empty tomb, the perplexed women encounter "two men... in gleaming bright clothing," heavenly messengers who deliver the resurrection news: "Why do you look for the living among the dead? He isn't here, but has been raised. Remember what he told you while he was still in Galilee, that the Human One must be handed over to sinners, be crucified, and on the third day rise again" (24:4-6). The women remember the words of Jesus and go to announce the resurrection to the apostles, but their report is dismissed as "nonsense" (24:11). Peter himself runs to the tomb and peers in to see the linen burial cloths lying empty. He "wonders" at what he sees but apparently is not yet fully believing.

A second appearance story—one unique to Luke's Gospel—takes place as two disciples leave the Jerusalem community and strike out on their own to the village of Emmaus (24:13-35). As they travel they are joined by the Risen Jesus, but they don't recognize him. When Jesus asks them the reason for their distress, their answer describes Jesus and his mission in terms that resonate with Luke's Gospel as a whole—namely, "The things about Jesus of Nazareth. Because of his powerful deeds and words, he was recognized by God and all the people as a prophet. But our chief priests and our leaders handed him over to be sentenced to death, and they crucified him. We had hoped he was the one who would redeem Israel" (24:19-21). Jesus himself then instructs them on the meaning of these events, reviewing the scriptures for them. Jesus was not only a prophet but the Messiah, one whom the scriptures testify had "to suffer these things and then enter into his glory" (24:26). Their recognition of Jesus' presence comes when he agrees to stay with them and breaks bread with them. Characteristic of Luke's Gospel, it is at a meal with Jesus and in the evocative gestures of blessing and breaking the bread, as at the Passover meal and the great feedings of the multitudes, that the disciples realize that he has triumphed over death. Their hearts inflamed, they return to Jerusalem and the rest of the apostles to report their experience, only to discover that the Risen Christ had already appeared to Simon (24:34).

A final resurrection appearance now takes place, apparently on the same evening (24:36-49). Jesus appears to the apostles in Jerusalem and to quell their fear and doubt shows them the wounds of his crucifixion in his hands and his feet. To further convince them of his living presence, he asks for food and eats a piece of broiled fish in their presence. In this manner the resurrection appearance story emphasizes that the Risen Christ is indeed the Jesus whom they knew and loved. It is significant that Luke highlights the wounds of Jesus—emblematic of his crucifixion—and his eating of food as signs of Jesus' presence. Eating and drinking with them (see Peter's words in Acts

61

10:41) recalls the Last Passover where Jesus had dined with his disciples and, through the breaking of the bread and the cup poured out, had spoken of his death as a giving of life for them. As he had done with the disciples on the way to Emmaus, so here the Risen Jesus explains the events of his death and resurrection in the light of the scriptures—"the Law from Moses, the Prophets, and the Psalms" (24:44). He also commissions the disciples to be his "witnesses" bringing the message of "a change of heart and life for the forgiveness of sins" to all nations, "beginning from Jerusalem" (24:47-48).

Without question, in Luke's perspective, the death of Jesus is vindicated by God through the events of the resurrection and its aftermath. God raises Jesus from the dead and thereby confirms his identity as God's prophet, God's Son, and God's Messiah. The very sufferings and death of Jesus on the cross are the culmination of Jesus' messianic mission as Savior and have the power to transform human life: the good thief is ushered into paradise, the centurion who crucified Jesus now acclaims him as God's Just One, the crowds who had witnessed his death now beat their breasts in repentance, the disciples who had proven weak and uncomprehending finally stand by the cross of Jesus, the women who were his faithful disciples become the first to proclaim Jesus' triumph over death, and the Emmaus disciples and the apostles huddled in the upper room have their sorrow and disillusionment turned into joy and belief. Through the death, resurrection, and ascension of Jesus, the Spirit of God will be unleashed on the world and the message of repentance and forgiveness of sins will reach to the ends of the earth.

The Gospel of John

The crucifixion and death of Jesus stand at the center of John's portrayal of the cosmic redemptive mission of Jesus.[59] Explicit references to the cross are confined to chapter 19 of the passion account yet awareness of the death of Jesus and its meaning permeate the entirety of John's narrative.

The Deep Logic of John's Theology of the Cross

One might speak of a "deep logic" that runs through John's Gospel, from the prologue through to the resurrection appearances of Jesus, and that "logic" is closely entwined with the significance of Jesus' death.[60] The God-given and

---

59. See the ensemble of major essays in Van Belle, *The Death of Jesus in the Fourth Gospel*; see also Senior, *The Passion of Jesus in the Gospel of John*.

60. See Senior, "The Death of Jesus as Sign," in Van Belle, *The Death of Jesus in the Fourth Gospel*, 271–91; see also Morgan-Wynne, *The Cross in the Johannine Writings*.

cosmic mission of Jesus, the Word made flesh, is to reveal God's redemptive love for the world. That love is expressed in both the words and deeds of Jesus. Because the heart of Jesus' message is God's redeeming love, the most eloquent and unimpeachable expression of that love is Jesus' death on the cross, which is in fact the ultimate realization of love—the laying down of one's life for the sake of another. Because the death of Jesus is the ultimate expression of God's love for the world, it becomes the completion of Jesus' mission and the source of his exaltation and triumphant return to his Father. That transcendent act of love on the part of Jesus, dynamically transmitted to the disciples through the power of the Spirit sent by the Risen and Exalted Christ, also becomes the measure of authentic discipleship and the rationale for the community's own mission to the world. The ultimate destiny of those who believe in Jesus is to share in the very communion and unity of love shared between Jesus and his Father.

The starting point for the unfolding of this underlying "logic" is found in the poetic prologue of John's Gospel (1:1-18), which portrays the origin of Jesus as the Word of God present in the recesses of the very life of God before time began. The Word both spoken by God and equivalent to God arcs into the created world—the *kosmos*—which in fact is patterned on the Word and fashioned through the Word. That "world" encompasses the human arena and is therefore able to both accept and reject God's Word. The ultimate immersion of the Word in the world is sealed when the Word "became flesh" (1:14), that is, became genuinely human in every respect. The prologue concludes by affirming that the fundamental purpose of the Word's presence in the world is to reveal the God "no one has ever seen" (1:18). In and through the flesh of the Word incarnate, the community is able to see the "glory" of God (1:14).

With the incarnate Word present and visible in the world, the profound questions posed by the gospel are, *What does the Word have to say? What is the mission given to the Word?* John's Gospel answers those questions in multiple ways throughout the narrative in both word and "sign [*sēmeion*]," the latter the term the Fourth Gospel uses for the miracles of Jesus.

The Words of Jesus

1. The "Lifting up" Sayings

The encounter with Nicodemus in John 3 is the first of several discourses in the gospel and here we find an explicit statement of the "Word's" God-given mission. Jesus speaks for first time of his being "lifted up" (*hypsōthēnai*), a reference to the incident in Numbers 21:4-9 where Moses is instructed by

God to hold up an image of the very serpent that had been afflicting the people as a paradoxical means of healing them (3:14). In John's creative manner the "lifting up" sayings become the equivalent to the Synoptic passion predictions. The term "lifted up" (*hypsōthēnai*) captures the unique perspective of John's theology of the cross—the Crucified Jesus is indeed "lifted up" on the cross but paradoxically that tortuous action becomes the means of Jesus' exaltation and triumphant return to his father. Contemplating the Crucified Jesus is a source of ultimate healing—eternal life itself—for those who believe in him. In the Son of Man's so being "lifted up" on the cross, "everyone who believes in him will have eternal life" (3:15).

The following well-known verses in this inaugural discourse drive home this message and are among John's most explicit statement of the redemptive mission of the Word: "God so loved the world that he gave his only Son, so that everyone who believes in him won't perish but will have eternal life. God didn't send his Son into the world to judge the world, but that the world might be saved through him" (3:16-17). Here is the lynchpin of John's theology of the death of Jesus. That death is not to be understood as a hideous defeat and repudiation of Jesus' mission but, paradoxically, the death of Jesus reveals God's love for the world and is the source of its salvation.

A second "lifting up" saying occurs in John 8:28. In a sharply polemical context Jesus challenges the religious leaders: "When the Human One is lifted up, then you will know that I Am. Then you will know that I do nothing on my own, but I say just what the Father has taught me. He who sent me is with me. He doesn't leave me by myself, because I always do what makes him happy" (8:28-29). Key elements of what we are calling the deep logic of John's overall theology are also present here. The death of Jesus that is inflicted on him by his opponents (literally, "When *you* have lifted up") paradoxically will reveal the divine presence embodied in Jesus—"you will know that I Am"—the divine name that Jesus, the incarnate Word, bears repeatedly in John's Gospel.[61] And his opponents will also come to realize that the Father is the one who sent Jesus into the world to reveal God's love for the world—a love expressed in ultimate terms by Jesus' laying down his life for his beloved.

A third such saying occurs in John 12, a key transition point between the public ministry of Jesus and the advent of the passion story. In a scene that appears to be John's equivalent to the Gethsemane prayer of the Synoptics, Jesus is "troubled" and contemplates asking his Father to deliver him from

61. See, e.g., John 6:20; 8:24, 28; 13:19; John will also couple the "I Am" sayings to key predicates such as "I am the bread of life" (6:35, 51)—see also 8:12; 9:5; 10:7, 9, 11, 14; 11:25; 14:6; 15:1, 5. On this feature of John's Gospel, see R. Brown, *The Gospel according to John I–XII*, 533–38.

"this time" (literally John uses the term "hour" [*hōra*] when referring to his death; 12:27-28). But the Johannine Jesus reaffirms his commitment to his God-given mission: "No, for this is the reason"—giving his life out of love for the world—"I have come to this " (literally, "hour"; 12:27). Jesus goes on to proclaim that through his life-giving death he will seal his ultimate victory over "this world's ruler"—another powerful motif of John's theology of the cross (12:31).[62] The third "lifting up" saying immediately follows: "When I am lifted up from the earth, I will draw everyone to me." The narrator makes the reference to Jesus' death explicit: "He said this to show how he was going to die" (12:32-33). This third saying highlights the cosmic impact of the triumphant death of Jesus. Through his death and exaltation, Jesus, the Word incarnate, reveals God's all-encompassing love for the world and triumphs over the power of evil and death.

2. The Other Discourses

In several of the discourses in John's Gospel, this fundamental affirmation of the salvific meaning of Jesus' mission is repeated. In the "bread of life" discourse in John 6, Jesus speaks of himself as "the living bread that came down from heaven" and goes on to state that "the bread that I will give for the life of the world is my flesh" (6:51)—a clear reference to his death. The one who eats this bread "will live forever." As in the prologue, the object of Jesus' saving mission is "for the life of the world."

Another example is in the discourse in John 7 that takes place in the context of the Feast of Tabernacles: "On the last and most important day of the festival, Jesus stood up and shouted, 'All who are thirsty should come to me! All who believe in me should drink!'" (7:37-38). John's Gospel goes on to explain that this was a reference to the Spirit that "those who believed in him would soon receive," but as yet there was no Spirit "since Jesus hadn't yet been glorified" (7:39). This is a reference to Jesus' death, which John's Gospel paradoxically characterizes as when Jesus would be "glorified."[63]

The "good shepherd" discourse in John 10 also anticipates the saving effect of Jesus' death. The very purpose of Jesus' mission is "so that they could have life—indeed, so that they could live life to the fullest" (10:10). In contrast to the "hired hand" who abandons the sheep in face of the attack of the wolves, Jesus declares, "I am the good shepherd. The good shepherd lays down his life for the sheep" (10:11, 15). This act of love and protection on Jesus' part is indeed his mission from his father: "This is why the Father loves

---

62. See below; pp. 67–69.

63. See, e.g., John 11:4; 12:16, 23, 28; 13:31, 32; 14:30; 17:10.

me: I give up my life so that I can take it up again. No one takes it from me, but I give it up because I want to. I have the right to give it up, and I have the right to take it up again. I received this commandment from my Father" (10:17-18).

Jesus' Signs

What is true of the discourses in their reference to the saving effects of Jesus' death as the heart of his mission is also true of the "signs" (*sēmeia*) that Jesus performs. The first of these signs takes place at the wedding feast of Cana and here, too, a link to Jesus' death is alluded to. His mother's request to come to the aid of the wedding hosts when the wine runs out is at first rebuffed by Jesus since his "*hour* had not yet come" (2:4 AT)—a distinctive Johannine manner of speaking of the death of Jesus.[64] Yet Jesus goes on to transform the water into abundant and excellent wine—a sign of transformation that alludes to the impact of his salvific death.

In John's sequence of events Jesus' prophetic action of cleansing the temple follows the sign at Cana and also contains a clear reference to his death. Jesus directly challenges those who oppose his action in the temple: "Destroy this temple, and in three days I'll raise it up," a comment explained by the narrator as a reference to the temple of his body, one that would be remembered by his disciples "after he was raised from the dead" (2:19-22).

Other signs of Jesus are also transformative: the healing of the royal official's son who "was about to die" (4:46-54); the healing of the paralyzed man at the pools of Bethesda (5:1-18), which also triggers deadly opposition to Jesus (5:18); the feeding of the multitudes (6:1-15); and the healing of the man born blind, which also ends in sharp controversy with the Jewish authorities (9:1-41).

The Raising of Lazarus as Climactic Sign

The final sign of Jesus' public ministry, the raising of Lazarus, has the most explicit connection to the meaning of Jesus' death (11:1-44). John underscores the fact that Jesus loves his friend Lazarus (11:3, 5, 11, 33-36, 38): Jesus is deeply distressed at the loss of Lazarus (11:33) and weeps for him (35). Jesus declares at the outset that the raising of his friend Lazarus from the dead will be "for the glory of God so that God's Son can be glorified through it" (11:4)—fulfilling the very purpose of Jesus' mission to reveal God's love

---

64. See especially, John 13:1-2; see also 2:4; 7:30; 8:20; 12:23, 27; 16:32; 17:1; 19:27; see further de La Potterie, *The Hour of Jesus.*

for the world. This single act of rescuing one whom Jesus loves from the power of death sums up the entire mission of Jesus—one expressed throughout the gospel in his words and deeds and one that will be explicitly affirmed in the final discourse and in the passion story itself (see 13:1; 15:13).[65]

At the same time, in John's schema, it is Jesus' action of saving the life of Lazarus that puts in motion the forces that will lead to Jesus' own death (see 11:54-57). Troubled by the impact of Jesus' raising of Lazarus, the chief priests and the Pharisees meet in council to decide what to do. They fear the consequences of Jesus performing his signs, "If we let him go on like this, everyone will believe in him. Then the Romans will come and take away both our temple and our people" (11:47-48). At this dramatic moment the High Priest Caiaphas makes his famous declaration that paves the way to Jesus' death on the cross: "You don't know anything! You don't see that it is better for you that one man die for the people rather than the whole nation be destroyed" (11:49-50). The narrator drives home the ironic significance of what Caiaphas says: "He didn't say this on his own. As high priest that year, he prophesied that Jesus would soon die for the nation—and not only for the nation. Jesus would also die so that God's children scattered everywhere would be gathered together as one" (11:51-52). Here John's Gospel explicitly states the saving impact of the death of Jesus.

Forces Leading to the Death of Jesus

The ultimate expression of Jesus' mission from the Father—the final "sign" as it were—will be the death of Jesus presented in the Passion Narrative itself.[66] John's Gospel recognizes other driving forces in the body of the gospel narrative that lead to the crucifixion of Jesus.[67] The Jewish religious authorities are among the prime movers.[68] Opposition to Jesus breaks out at the very beginning of the gospel narrative at the cleansing of the temple (2:18-20), intensifies after John 4 and comes to the boiling point in the aftermath of the raising of Lazarus when the Pharisees and the chief priests

---

65. On this motif as the key to Johannine theology, see especially Moloney, *Love in the Gospel of John*.

66. Dodd, *The Interpretation of the Fourth Gospel*, 438–39.

67. On this see Koester, "Why Was the Messiah Crucified?," in Van Belle, *The Death of Jesus in the Fourth Gospel*, 163–80.

68. As is well known, John usually refers to the authorities as simply "the Jews"—a problematic generalization that enabled the opposition to Jesus portrayed in the Gospel of John to be used as a rationale for anti-Semitism. Our focus here is on the theological interpretation of the death of Jesus on the cross as presented in John, but we cannot be indifferent to the collateral damage caused over the centuries by John's designation of the human opposition to Jesus by the Jewish leaders. On this issue, see Bieringer, Pollefeyt, and Vandecastelle-Vanneuville, *Anti-Judaism and the Fourth Gospel*.

decide to arrest Jesus and have him put to death (11:53). The intent to "kill" Jesus on the part of the religious leaders occurs several times in John's account and gives the opposition to Jesus a particularly bitter edge (see 5:14; 7:1, 19, 25; 8:22, 37, 40).

The Romans, too, become part of the human agency that causes the death of Jesus. Pilate is portrayed in John—as he is in all four of the Gospels—as initially reluctant to condemn Jesus and even struck with fear in the presence of Jesus and the claim attributed to him to be "God's Son" (19:7). But despite his repeated attempts to release Jesus, Pilate ultimately succumbs to expediency, especially when the leaders raise the ante by suggesting that releasing Jesus would make Pilate no friend of the emperor because of Jesus' supposed claims to be a king who "opposes the emperor" (19:12). The tug of war with the Jewish leaders ends with Pilate "[handing] over Jesus to them to be crucified" (19:16). Roman troops carry out Jesus' crucifixion and, at the request of the religious leaders and agreed to by Pilate, ensure that Jesus and those crucified with him are dead before the onset of the Sabbath, which in John's timetable is also the beginning of the Passover festival (19:31-37).

John's Gospel also sees the power of Satan as a driving force leading to the death of Jesus.[69] In contrast to the Synoptic Gospels, John's account does not portray Jesus as an exorcist. Rather, Satan lurks behind the scenes, fomenting hatred, encouraging deception and lying, and driving humans to oppose and ultimately attempting to destroy Jesus, God's messenger.[70] This is clear in the bitter confrontation between Jesus and his opponents in John 8. John's Gospel interprets their failure to listen to Jesus and inability to understand what he says as a result of the sway of Satan over them: "Your father is the devil. You are his children, and you want to do what your father wants. He was a murderer from the beginning. He has never stood for the truth, because there's not truth in him. Whenever that liar speaks, he speaks according to this own nature, because he's a liar and the father of liars" (8:44).

Judas in particular is portrayed as an instrument of the devil. In John 6:70-71, Jesus states to Simon Peter and the disciples: "'Didn't I choose you twelve? Yet one of you is a devil.' He was speaking of Judas, Simon Iscariot's son for he, one of the Twelve, was going to betray him." The reader had already learned after Judas had protested Mary's generous anointing of Jesus' feet at Bethany that Judas, who held the common purse, was in fact a thief (12:4-6). John follows through with this on the eve of Jesus' death when

---

69. See earlier, chap. 2, pp. 22–23.
70. On this see, Koester, "Why Was the Messiah Crucified?," 170.

at the Last Supper he notes, "The devil had already provoked Judas, Simon Iscariot's son, to betray Jesus" (13:2). Later during the Supper John puts the spotlight once more on Judas's betrayal. Jesus laments, "I assure you, one of you will betray me" (13:21). Jesus indicates to the Beloved Disciple (at Peter's request) who the betrayer is: "'It's the one who to whom I will give this piece of bread once I have dipped into the bowl.' Then he dipped the piece of bread and gave it to Judas, Simon Iscariot's son. After Judas received the bread from Jesus"—a sign of friendship—"Satan entered into him" (13:26-27).

Although John's Gospel will not refer again in his narrative to the explicit role of Satan as the cause of Jesus' death, it is clear that through the agency of both the religious leaders who virulently oppose Jesus and through the betrayal of Judas, one of the Twelve, Satan will assault Jesus with deadly force. Yet Jesus' obedient giving of his life out of love for the world and his resurrection and triumphant exaltation signal the radical defeat of the power of darkness. Satan, "this world's ruler" will be condemned (16:11). With Jesus' death on the cross, "now is the time [literally, "hour"] for judgment of this world. Now this world's ruler will be thrown out" (12:31).

John 13–17: The Farewell Discourse

John's theology of the death of Jesus finds its full expression in his account of the death of Jesus. John prefaces the Passion Narrative itself with Jesus' long farewell discourse, where he instructs his disciples at the meal on the eve of Passover (John 13–17). Here some of the most characteristic motifs of John's theology find expression, including those that throw light on the meaning of Jesus' death.

John portrays Jesus as fully conscious that he is about to complete his mission and repeatedly refers to his return to the Father (see 13:1-2, 3, 33, 36; 14:1-14, 18, 28; 16:5-11, 16-18, 28). This motif of Jesus' return to his Father crescendos in John 17, the so-called high priestly prayer of Jesus, which brings the final discourse to its conclusion.

The ultimate intent of Jesus' mission is clearly stated at the very beginning of the farewell discourse that is also the opening of the so-called book of glory—the latter half of the Gospel of John that focuses on the passion of Jesus—"Before the Festival of Passover, Jesus knew that his time [i.e., his "hour"] had come to leave this world and go to the Father. Having loved his own who were in the world, he loved them fully [literally: "unto the end"; *eis telos*]" (13:1). The phrase "to the end" (*eis telos*) connects directly with the final words of Jesus in John's Passion Narrative: as death comes, Jesus exclaims, "It is completed" (19:30; *tetelestai*)—the Greek term identical to the root

69

word "end" (*telos*) in 13:1. With his death Jesus "completes" the mission of revealing God's love to the world.

Other allusions to the saving power of Jesus' death appear in this segment of John's account. John relates the death of Jesus to the Passover festival. At the beginning of the gospel John the Baptist had identified Jesus as "the Lamb of God who takes away the sin of the world" (1:29), connecting Jesus and his mission to the sacrifice of the Passover lamb.[71] As the death of Jesus approaches, John signals its timing with the Passover (11:55; 12:1; 13:1). Jesus' death will coincide with the slaughter of the lambs in preparation for the Passover festival (19:14, 31; also noted at the burial of Jesus in 19:42), and the Crucified Jesus is spared having his bones broken by the soldiers, which the gospel notes fulfills the scriptures that *"they won't break any of his bones,"* (19:36), an instruction that Exodus 12:46 gives concerning the lamb prepared for the Passover.[72] Like the Exodus event that Passover commemorated, the death of Jesus liberates the world from the power of sin and death.

The foot washing that is unique to John's Gospel also seems entwined with the meaning of Jesus' death as an act of total self-transcendence and humble service (13:3-11), not unlike the Synoptic interpretation of the meaning of Jesus' death.[73] Jesus realizes that the imminent completion of his mission is at hand—"Jesus knew the Father had given everything into his hands and that he had come from God and was returning to God" (13:3)—and this prompts the act of washing the feet of his disciples, an eloquent sign of Jesus' mission of humble service to others. At the conclusion of the gesture Jesus speaks again of his betrayer and his impending death (13:18-19).

Another vivid symbol is Jesus' reference to his death as giving birth. Jesus consoles the disciples in their distress about his speaking of leaving them. Their "sorrow will turn into joy" just as a woman who is in labor experiences pain "because her time [literally, "her hour"] has come. But when the child is born, she no longer remembers her distress because of her joy that a child has been born into the world" (16:20-21). In the same way the sadness of the disciples at Jesus' departure in death will be turned into joy in the triumph of his resurrection and his return to the Father (16:22). Some interpreters have drawn a link between this metaphor of childbirth to explain the life-giving meaning of Jesus' death and the words of Jesus to his mother and the Beloved

---

71. On this motif, see Porter, "Can Traditional Exegesis Enlighten Literary Analysis of the Fourth Gospel?," in Evans and Stegner, *The Gospels and the Scriptures of Israel*, 396–428; Koester, *Symbolism in the Fourth Gospel*, 216–24.

72. See Senior, *The Passion of Jesus in the Gospel of John*, 122.

73. See earlier, pp. 54–56. The resemblance to the discourse in Luke's account (22:27) is striking.

Disciple from the cross (19:25-27). Through the death of Jesus a new family is born.[74]

Most significant of all are Jesus' instructions about the love command in John 15:9-17 since here the words of Jesus tie into the fundamental purpose of his mission stated at the outset of the gospel and relate it explicitly to the meaning of his death. The disciples are told to "love each other" in the same manner as Jesus has loved them (15:12). That love finds its fullest expression and its most compelling example in the willingness "to give up one's life for one's friends" (15:13). Here in Johannine terms is the full meaning of Jesus' death on the cross. Those who oppose Jesus and have sought to kill him and the Romans who out of expediency condemn him to crucifixion view the cross as a way of silencing Jesus and nullifying the threat he might pose—this is the hatred of the "world" directed at Jesus and his followers in its most negative manifestation (see 15:18-19; 16:2).[75] But from Jesus' own vantage point and from that of the God who sent him into the world, his death on the cross is an unimpeachable act of love, one that can heal the world and transform it from death to life.

John 18–19: The Passion Narrative

While John's account is truly a Passion Narrative—Jesus is arrested, interrogated, tortured, condemned, and crucified on the cross—it also has a triumphant tone unmatched in the Synoptic versions. This "triumphant" mood of John's passion story itself already implies the saving impact of his death.[76]

Jesus as King

John gives special attention to the role of Jesus as "king" in the Passion Narrative. Jesus is ironically proclaimed "king of the Jews" by Pilate, he is mocked as such by the soldiers, Jesus' claim to kingship is affixed in all the languages of the Roman world to his cross, and Jesus will be given a royal burial by Joseph of Arimathea in a "new tomb" and his crucified body lavishly

74. Koester, *Symbolism in the Fourth Gospel*, 241–44; Senior, *The Passion of Jesus in the Gospel of John*, 108–14. See also R. Brown, *The Gospel according to John XIII–XXI*, 925-26, who also connects this scene to Cana where Jesus also addressed his mother as "woman" and referred to his "hour" (see John 2:1-11).

75. John uses the term "world" (*kosmos*) in multiple senses: as the world of humanity created in the pattern of the Logos (1:10), as the object of the Father's redemptive love (3:16-17), as the neutral arena of human existence (into which one "come[s] into the world" and "leave[s] the world"; 9:39; 13:1), but also as the world of opposition to Jesus and the disciples (17:14).

76. Not unlike the manner in which the apocalyptic signs that follow immediately upon the death of Jesus already anticipate the resurrection; see Matt 27:51-55.

anointed with a mixture of myrrh and aloes "nearly seventy-five pounds in all" (19:38-42).[77]

This motif ties in to John's emphasis both on the cosmic significance of Jesus' mission and the conviction that through his mission of revealing God's love for the world, Jesus radically defeats the power of death in all its expressions. As noted above, John's Gospel portrays Satan, the "prince of darkness" and the "father of lies," as mortally opposed to Jesus and his mission.[78] Expressed through the bitter hostility of Jesus' opponents (8:43-51), the betrayal of his own disciple Judas (13:2), and the cynical expedience of Roman authority, Satan attempts to thwart Jesus' God-given mission to reveal the truth: God loves the world and will not condemn it.

Satan's final assault is the crucifixion of Jesus itself. But in the dramatic paradox understood by John's Gospel, the crucifixion and death of Jesus as the supreme expression of love is the very means through which Jesus' mission is completed![79] Therefore "this world's ruler" is condemned (16:11), and through his death Jesus has triumphed over the world ruled by evil (16:33).

The Death of Jesus as "Completion"

As noted earlier, John frames his account of the passion with references to the "completion" of Jesus' work, both at the beginning of the book of glory— "Having loved his own who were in the world, he loved them fully" (or, literally, "unto the end," in the Greek, *eis ton telon*; 13:1)—and in the final words of Jesus before his death—"It is completed" (19:30). Both sayings of Jesus utilize the root word, *teleō*, meaning to "finish" or "complete."

Through the death of Jesus, John affirms, the cosmic mission of Jesus comes full circle. The death of Jesus on the cross is both the climax of Jesus' earthly mission and the catalyst for his triumphant return to God. This cosmic journey and its center point in the death of Jesus effect human salvation. The revelation of God's redeeming love for the world is not casual knowledge but is radically transformative. To intimately know God's love, to experience it through the revelation of the incarnate Word, is to make one reborn (1:12-13; see also the discussion with Nicodemus in 3:3). God's love, in the convic-

---

77. Most commentators interpret the extraordinary amount of spices used in the anointing of Jesus as symbolic of his royal status; see, e.g., Koester, *Symbolism in the Fourth Gospel*, 227–30.

78. See previously, pp. 68–69.

79. Note the ironic comments of Caiphas in John 11:50—"it is better for you that one man die for the people rather than the whole nation be destroyed"—and the narrator's reflection, "He didn't say this on his own. As high priest that year, he prophesied that Jesus would soon die for the nation—and not only for the nation. Jesus would also die so that God's children scattered everywhere would be gathered together as one" (11:51-52).

tion of John's theology, creates a new human being, free from fear and radical death and bathed in the light (3:21; 9:5, 39). As Jesus' vivid image in the farewell discourse had foretold, through the pain of his death a new life has been born into the world (16:21).

The Signs that Follow the Death of Jesus

John's Gospel underscores the impact of Jesus' death through the remarkable signs that accompany it. To ensure that Jesus and those crucified with him are dead and removed from the cross prior to the onset of the Passover and the Sabbath (19:31), the soldiers break the legs of those crucified with Jesus, but, since he was already dead, they do not break Jesus' legs. As noted above, John sees in this a link between the Passover lamb and the Crucified Jesus (19:36)—Jesus is the "Lamb of God" who through the sacrifice of his life out of love "takes away the sins of the world" (1:29).[80] The fulfillment of the quotation from Exodus 12:46 (see also Num 9:12) about not breaking the bones of the Passover lamb seals the connection.

But the decision to refrain from breaking the bones of Jesus also prompts one of the soldiers to ensure Jesus is dead by thrusting a lance into his side—an act unique to John's Gospel (19:34). John clearly sees great significance in the blood and water that flow from Jesus' wound; the testimony of an eyewitness—the Beloved Disciple?—alerts the reader that these signs have profound meaning: "The one who saw this has testified, and his testimony is true. He knows that he speaks the truth, and he has testified so that you also can believe" (19:35). As is often the case with John's Gospel, the precise meaning of such signs is not always self-evident. The symbolic meaning of the water may be the most evident since John has explicitly connected water with the presence of the Spirit. The discourse with Nicodemus links water and the Spirit: "Unless someone is born of water and the Spirit, it's not possible to enter God's kingdom" (3:5)—a probable reference to baptism.[81] The link between Jesus and life-giving water is made again in Jesus' dialogue with the Samaritan woman. Jesus presents himself as giving living water: "Whoever drinks from the water that I will give will never be thirsty again. The water that I give will become in those who drink it a spring of water that bubbles up into eternal life" (4:14).

An explicit link between water, the Spirit, and the death of Jesus also occurs in John 7:37-39. The narrator explains that Jesus' reference to "rivers of living water" was, in fact, a reference to the Spirit: "Those who believed in

---

80. See earlier, p. 70.

81. Koester, *Symbolism in the Fourth Gospel*, 175–206.

him would soon receive the Spirit, but they hadn't experienced the Spirit yet since Jesus hadn't yet been glorified" (7:39)—the latter a reference in Johannine terms to the death of Jesus.[82] In his farewell discourse Jesus had repeatedly referred to the gift of the Paraclete, who would come into the world in the aftermath of Jesus' death and exaltation (see 14:25-26; 16:7-11). In John's perspective, the Spirit/Paraclete will enable the disciples to remember and understand the teaching of Jesus and will provide the strength to complete Jesus' mission of overcoming evil and revealing God's love for the world. The Risen Christ breathes the Spirit upon his disciples and gives them the power to forgive sins (20:22-23). Thus through the sign of water flowing from the open side of Jesus, John affirms that the death of Jesus brings upon the disciples the life-giving Spirit that will enable them to carry out their mission to the world.

The flow of blood is also a potent symbol of the saving power of Jesus' death on the cross. To decipher the precise meaning of *blood* in this context, some commentators appeal to the First Letter of John where blood is linked both to water and to the Spirit: "This is one who came by water and blood: Jesus Christ. Not by water only but by water and blood. And the Spirit is the one who testifies, because the Spirit is the truth. The three are testifying—the Spirit, the water, and the blood—and the three are united in agreement" (1 John 5:6-8). Blood then would signify—along with the water of baptism and the gift of the Spirit—the saving significance of Jesus' death.

In the "bread of life" discourse, John's Gospel as well refers several times to the blood of Jesus as expressive of the saving power of Jesus' death. In the idiom of this discourse the body and blood of Jesus are vital nourishment that the believer must imbibe in order to truly live: "Whoever eats my flesh and drinks my blood has eternal life, and I will raise them up at the last day." (6:54; see also 6:53, 55-56). The eating and drinking metaphor of the discourse refers most immediately to union with Jesus through faith, although a reference to the Eucharist cannot be ruled out.[83] Similarly, *flesh* and *blood* refer to the very presence of the Word incarnate, with whom the believer is united through faith. John connects this set of metaphors to the death of Jesus in the key verse of 6:51: "The bread I will give for the life of the world is my flesh." The "bread of life" that Jesus gives and that the believer shares in through eating and drinking the "flesh and blood" of Jesus is most manifest in the death of Jesus, which is "for the life of the world."

---

82. There is some ambiguity about Jesus' saying here, including its punctuation and whether the "living water" flows from Jesus or from the one who believes in him (see the discussion in Moloney, *The Gospel of John*, 252–53). In any case the link between water and Spirit and the death of Jesus remains intact.

83. See the discussion in R. Brown, *The Gospel according to John I–XII*, 284–94, who concludes that a reference to the Eucharist is most probable.

John concludes the scene of Jesus' death with a quotation from Zechariah 12:10: "They will look at him whom they have pierced." Who are the ones that the quotation now refers to as "they"—the soldiers? Jesus' opponents? Jesus' mother and the Beloved Disciple? The sister of the mother of Jesus, Mary the wife of Clopas, and Mary Magdalene? (see 19:25)—John does not identify those who look on "the one whom they pierced." It is also not clear whether the first "they" is identical to the second—implying that the ones who now observe Jesus are the same as those who crucified him.

Equally uncertain is the implied tone of the quotation—in what spirit do these onlookers now view the crucified body of Jesus? The original quotation from Zechariah provides a tantalizing hint although the precise circumstances of Zechariah's oracle and its reference to one "whom they pierced" are very uncertain. What is clear is that in viewing the offense or injury caused, the people of Jerusalem mourn what they have done, earning God's compassion. Does John want to imply the same here in the wake of Jesus' death? Like the crowds in Luke's Gospel who beat their breasts in repentance in witnessing the death of the righteous one (see 23:48), those who witness the death of Jesus and the life-giving signs that flow from his pierced body are repentant and, thereby, receive God's compassionate forgiveness.[84]

That transforming impact of the death of Jesus might also be in play in the burial scene that immediately follows: Joseph of Arimathea, whose discipleship was kept secret "out of fear," now comes forward to claim the body of Jesus, and Nicodemus, a would-be disciple who had first approached Jesus "by night," now openly brings an abundance of spices to anoint the body of his Lord (see 19:38-42). The death of Jesus brings transformation and new life.

Resurrection Signs

Because his passion account has a triumphant resurrection tone, the discovery of the empty tomb and the resurrection appearances that conclude John's narrative have a certain anticlimactic tone. Their point is less to affirm the resurrection of Jesus than it is to show its impact on the disciples.

A key character is Mary Magdalene, who is the first to discover the empty tomb (John 20:1-10). Since Jesus' body was already lavishly anointed (19:39-40), she seems to come to the tomb out of devotion, continuing her vigil

---

84. See, e.g., Forestell, *The Word of the Cross*, 89–90. R. Brown, while conceding that the original context of the Zechariah quotation speaks of God's compassion, does not think that applies here. He suggests that two different groups are the ones "looking on"; on the one hand the opponents of Jesus are being judged as they stand at the cross, while the Beloved Disciple and the faithful women are seeing a sign of redemption. See *The Gospel according to John XIII–XXI*, 953–56.

begun at the cross (19:25). Mary brings the news to the disciples, and Peter and the Beloved Disciple run to the tomb (the Beloved Disciple outruns Peter!). Peter observes the linen wrappings that had enshrouded Jesus' crucified body and the cloth that had covered his face "folded up in its own place" (20:7). Faith begins to dawn in the Beloved Disciple although John notes "they didn't yet understand the scripture that Jesus must rise from the dead" (20:9).

Peter and the Beloved Disciple return to their homes but Mary maintains her sorrowful vigil by the tomb. But now her grief will be turned into joy and a sense of mission—another sign of the transformation effected by Jesus' dying and rising. She first sees two angels present where Jesus' body had laid and then, in one of the Fourth Gospel's most exquisite and tender scenes, she encounters the Risen Jesus himself (20:14). Characteristic notes of John's theology are in place: Mary is not to grasp Jesus because his return to his Father ("to my Father and your Father, to my God and your God" [20:17]) is not yet complete. With that, Mary is charged to bring the news of the resurrection to the disciples, earning her the unique title in the early church—"missionary to the apostles."[85]

Now "that evening" the disciples themselves receive an appearance of the Risen Christ (20:19-23). Once again the impact of the death and resurrection of Jesus is to turn the disciples' fear—they were behind locked doors "because they were afraid of the Jewish authorities"—into joy and empowerment. Jesus greets them with "peace" and breathes the Spirit on them, giving them the power to forgive sins. The connection to the death of Jesus is made explicit: the Risen Jesus still bears the wounds of his crucifixion and these will remain a focus in the scene that follows. Thomas's hesitation enables John's Gospel to underscore the fact that the death of Jesus on the cross was itself part of the saving power now evident in the experience of resurrection. Invited to touch the wounds in the hands and side of the Risen Christ, Thomas is able to realize that through the death of Jesus, God's love for the world, which creates new life, has been made manifest. Thomas's response is one of the most explicit confessional statements in all of the New Testament: "My Lord and my God!" (20:28). What Thomas confesses when encountering in such a vivid way the Crucified and Risen Jesus is what future generations of believers will proclaim through the power of the Spirit.

John's Gospel concludes with a lovely resurrection appearance story that takes place in Galilee (21:1-23). Because the gospel seems to formally con-

---

85. Mary's prominent role reflects John's tendency to highlight prominent women characters in his narrative; see Fehribach, *The Women in the Life of the Bridegroom*.

clude at the end of chapter 20, interpreters have speculated that chapter 21 is a later addition to the gospel.[86] However, it, too, continues the message of the transforming impact of the death and resurrection of Jesus. Peter's threefold denial of Jesus in the Passion Narrative (18:15-18, 25-27) is transformed by the Risen Jesus into a threefold declaration of love (21:15-19). Peter is not only forgiven his denial of his master but is given the mission to "feed my lambs," "feed my sheep." As was true for Mary Magdalene at the tomb and the disciples in the locked room, the Crucified and Risen Jesus transforms Peter's fear and grief into a new relationship with him and a new mission in his name.

Conclusion

In multiple ways, the four gospels proclaim that the cross of Jesus is the culmination of his mission to save humanity from the devastating power of sin and death. The cross becomes the paradoxical expression of God's redeeming love for the world, transforming a heinous instrument of death and destruction into a sign of eternal life and liberation.

---

86. There are, however, no extant ancient manuscripts that do not include John 21. On this issue, see R. Brown, *The Gospel according to John XIII–XXI*, 1077–82.

Chapter Four

Paul and the Saving Power of the Cross

Attempting to describe what the cross as a source of salvation means in Paul's theology is equivalent to describing the entirety of Paul's message. Our limited scope does not permit attempting such a full review, so we will focus on some of the key elements of Paul's theology of the cross.[1] In this section we will concentrate on the seven letters of unquestioned Pauline authorship; a later segment will take up key passages from the so-called deuteropauline literature.[2] Given its dominant role in Paul's theological vision, the specific word "cross" (*stauros*) or other adjectival or verbal forms of the word ("crucified," "to crucify") occur less frequently than one might expect and do not appear at all in Romans, Paul's most expansive letter.[3] However, Paul speaks frequently of the death of Jesus or the sufferings of Jesus and in virtually every instance he has in mind Jesus' death on the *cross*, including multiple such references in the Letter to the Romans.[4]

1. Helpful overviews of Pauline theology can be found in Dunn, *The Theology of Paul the Apostle*; Gorman, *Apostle of the Crucified Lord*; Schnelle, *Apostle Paul*; Wright, *Paul and the Faithfulness of God*. Particularly helpful for Paul's theology of the cross, see Cousar, *A Theology of the Cross*.

2. The undisputed letters include: Romans, 1 and 2 Corinthians, Galatians, Philippians, 1 Thessalonians, and Philemon.

3. The noun "cross" (*stauros*) referring to the cross of Christ occurs seven times in the undisputed letters (1 Cor 1:17, 18; Gal 5:11; 6:12, 14; Phil 2:8; 3:18). Other forms of the word applied to the death of Jesus appear in 1 Cor 1:13, 23; 2:2, 8; 2 Cor 13:4; Gal 3:1; 5:24; 6:14. The term "crucify with" (*systauroō*) occurs in Rom 6:6; Gal 2:19.

4. See Rom 5:10; 6:3, 5, 8, 9, 10; 8:34.

Influenced by the diverse contexts of his letters and the issues of concern to the community he is addressing, Paul uses a variety of metaphors and terminology to express the meaning of Jesus' death on the cross. Underneath those diverse expressions, however, some fundamental convictions of Paul arch through all of his writings, and it is this fundamental perspective we want to capture.

For Paul, as for the entirety of the New Testament, Jesus' death on the cross is essentially linked to his triumph over death through his resurrection. Paul himself states this in blunt terms in his extended reflection on resurrection in 1 Corinthians 15: "If Christ hasn't been raised, then your faith is worthless; you are still in your sins, and what's more, those who have died in Christ are gone forever. If we have a hope in Christ only in this life, then we deserve to be pitied more than anyone else" (vv. 17-19). Without resurrection, the cross of Christ becomes a tragic symbol—signifying the ultimate triumph of death over one who claimed to be God's own Son and the Messiah sent to redeem the world. Without the resurrection, as Paul notes, the Christian message is a sham and those who have put their faith in it are to be pitied.

While the resurrection of the Crucified Jesus is essential for the saving power of the cross, Paul puts more emphatic focus on the *cross* of Jesus as the eloquent and startling revelation of God's very nature and the extraordinary way God effects human redemption. For Paul and his Jewish heritage, which he prized, the possibility of resurrection was not unexpected, but the reality of the cross was truly not anticipated—certainly not for God's Messiah. Thus the cross of Jesus becomes Paul's focus, without ever severing its essential connection to the resurrection of Christ.

I. The Death of Jesus on the Cross as Paul's Fundamental Vantage Point

There are many entry points one can take in trying to grasp the complex and multidimensional theological vision of Paul the apostle. Yet the death of Jesus on the cross is the lens through which Paul reflects on all of reality and therefore stands at the very center of his theology.

Recent Pauline studies have emphasized the "Jewishness" of Paul.[5] Rather than consider Paul as abandoning his Jewish heritage and turning to an en-

---

5. See, e.g., Schnelle, *Apostle Paul*, 70–75, who emphasizes the Jewish context of Paul's life and thought; Wright sees Paul's Jewish worldview "informing and undergirding him at every point," even though his encounter with Christ also causes him to rethink everything; see *Paul and the Faithfulness of God*, 354.

tirely new religious persuasion, interpreters of Paul stress a fundamental continuity in Paul's religious journey. At the same time there is disruption and change caused by his faith in Christ. As Paul himself notes in his Letter to the Philippians, his Jewish "pedigree" is strong:

> If anyone else has reason to put their confidence in physical advantages, I have even more:
> I was circumcised on the eighth day.
> I am from the people of Israel and the tribe of Benjamin.
> I am a Hebrew of the Hebrews.
> With respect to observing the Law, I'm a Pharisee.
> With respect to devotion to the faith, I harassed the church.
> With respect to righteousness under the Law, I'm blameless. (Phil 3:4-6)

In describing his "call" to be an apostle, Paul does not use the dramatic terms of his encounter with the Risen Christ on the road to Damascus found in Luke's account in Acts but evokes the prophetic reflections of Isaiah and Jeremiah that God had destined this for him before he was knit together in his mother's womb (Gal 1:15; see Isa 49; Jer 1). Paul thinks of his experience less as a conversion from one religious tradition to another than as a God-given "call" to a new role within the saga of salvation history.[6]

At the same time, Paul's experience of the Crucified and Risen Christ brings about a profound new perspective on Paul's part. Both Paul's autobiographical account in Galatians and Luke's dramatic narrative in Acts fundamentally agree that Paul had a visionary experience in which he encountered the Crucified Jesus as now the Risen and Exalted Christ. As Paul notes, "He [God] was pleased to reveal his Son to me" (Gal 1:15-16), and after citing the fundamental creedal formula of 1 Corinthians 15:3-4—"Christ died for our sins in line with the scriptures, he was buried, and he rose on the third day in line with the scriptures"—Paul goes on to note that the Crucified and Risen Christ also "appeared to me" (1 Cor 15:8).

The startling and unanticipated fact that the God of Israel and the creator of the world would choose as the anointed one and promised redeemer one who was crucified exploded into Paul's consciousness and forced him to look with new eyes at every aspect of his religious heritage and profound Jewish faith.[7] Paul did not discover Christ because he was frustrated with the law or

---

6. Krister Stendahl was influential in making this point; see Stendahl, *Paul among Jews and Gentiles*, 7–23.

7. Schnelle, *Apostle Paul*, 434; see also Wright, *Paul and the Faithfulness of God*, who notes that through his encounter with the fact of a Crucified Messiah, Paul's entire worldview "was simultaneously affirmed and transformed, destroyed and rebuilt" (563).

was disillusioned with Jewish practice.[8] Quite the contrary, by his own testimony Paul was exceptionally zealous, which led him to violently oppose the Christian movement as some kind of threat to Jewish orthodoxy—a stance that remained a constant embarrassment for Paul in his later life.[9] But his unanticipated encounter with the Crucified and Risen Christ—his "call" to proclaim this Crucified Christ as the Messiah of God—was the "solution" that made him see his "plight" in an entirely new way.[10] Discovering something new and wondrous made him aware of what he had not previously realized. Encountering a Crucified Christ drove Paul to rethink everything and to come to a new and startling awareness of the God of Israel who had always been present.

This is the key testimony that Paul gives his community in the famous opening passage of 1 Corinthians. Distressed by the rival and quarreling factions that had formed in the church at Corinth—something that Paul found incompatible with the faith that should bind them together—the apostle reaches for his fundamental belief in a Crucified Christ. There one finds a wisdom that is radically different than the world's wisdom, a flawed wisdom encouraging self-promotion and aggrandizement. But the authentic wisdom of God—a wisdom that calls for self-transcendence and a stance completely at odds with factionalism—is revealed in the cross of Christ. This passage is so key to understanding Paul's logic that it should be quoted in full:

> The message of the cross is foolishness to those who are being destroyed. But it is the power of God for those of us who are being saved. It is written in scripture: *I will destroy the wisdom of the wise, and I will reject the intelligence of the intelligent.* Where are the wise? Where are the legal experts? Where are today's debaters? Hasn't God made the wisdom of the world foolish? In God's wisdom, he determined that the world wouldn't come to know him through its wisdom. Instead, God was pleased to save those who believe through the foolishness of preaching. Jews ask for signs, and Greeks look for wisdom, but we preach Christ crucified, which is a scandal to Jews and foolishness to Gentiles. But to those who are called—both Jews and Greeks—Christ is God's power and God's wisdom. This is because the foolishness of God is wiser than human wisdom, and the weakness of God is stronger than human strength. (1 Cor 1:18-25)

---

8. That Paul agonized over his ability to be faithful to the law was the thesis of Richard Rubenstein who saw in Paul his own liberation from scrupulousness by means of psychoanalysis! See *My Brother Paul.*

9. See Gal 1:13-14, 22-23; Phil 3:6. We don't know for sure Paul's exact reason for persecuting the early Christians but it must have resulted from his perception that the Christians were errant in considering the Crucified Jesus as the Messiah and possibly for their relativizing of some aspects of law observance.

10. On this see Sanders, *Paul and Palestinian Judaism,* 442–47; On the other hand, Frank Thielman claims that Paul, along with all Jews in the Roman period, considered themselves under the curse of the law and that some critique of Jewish legalism can be found in Paul; see *From Plight to Solution.*

Here Paul lays out a conviction that informs his entire theology. That God would work in the world through a crucified human being, a human being who is in fact God's Son and liberating Messiah, is a truth so radical, so unexpected, and so profound in its implications that it confounds human wisdom. Neither the accumulated wisdom of Jewish religious experience nor the rational wisdom of the Greek philosophical world could conceive of God in such terms. But for Paul the reality of the Crucified and Risen Christ would become the key to understanding God's own unique wisdom and would therefore become the central message he would proclaim. As he reminds the Corinthians:

> When I came to you, brothers and sisters, I didn't come preaching God's secrets to you like I was an expert in speech or wisdom. I had made up my mind not to think about anything while I was with you except Jesus Christ, and to preach him as crucified. I stood in front of you with weakness, fear, and a lot of shaking. My message and my preaching weren't presented with convincing wise words but with a demonstration of the Spirit and of power. I did this so that your faith might not depend on the wisdom of people but on the power of God. (1 Cor 2:1-5)

II. God Confounds Human Wisdom and Reveals Power in Weakness

Jesus' death on the cross prompts Paul to discover anew the God of Israel, a God who confounds human wisdom and whose power is revealed in weakness. Paul's fundamental conviction that the Crucified and Risen Jesus was God's Messiah sent to redeem the world made him reimage his understanding of the God of Israel, the God that Paul had worshipped all his life but was now coming to know in a new and startling way. Put in its most basic terms, in choosing a Crucified Messiah God is revealed as one who works through what the world considers weakness. Instead of fitting into normal human expectations that a messenger of the almighty God would be perfect in form and circumstance, overcoming opposition and glorified in victory, God chooses a messenger who experiences one of the most repulsive and horrible fates that could inflict a human being. To be crucified meant one was condemned and rejected, one's cause, defeated and disdained.[11]

What kind of God worked through such "weakness"? Paul addresses this radical paradox at several points in his letters, often turning to his own

---

11. See earlier, pp. 5–6.

experience and that of his communities to offer some explanation. In 1 Corinthians, for example, Paul reminds his community that judged by ordinary human standards they themselves were not particularly "wise" or "powerful" or "upper class." In giving them the message of salvation, the God of Jesus Crucified was being true to God's paradoxical logic: "But God chose what the world considers foolish to shame the wise. God chose what the world considers weak to shame the strong. And God chose what the world considers low-class and low-life—what is considered to be nothing—to reduce what is considered to be something to nothing. So no human being can brag in God's presence" (1 Cor 1:27-29). In using such terms as "foolish," "weak," "low," and "considered to be nothing" Paul is surely thinking not only of the social standing of the Corinthians but of the Crucified Jesus himself.

The assertion in this passage from 1 Corinthians that God "chose...what is considered to be nothing...to reduce what is considered to be something to nothing" is echoed in an important chapter in Romans where Paul reflects on the experience of Abraham. Abraham, Paul asserts, was declared righteous by God not based on works of the law. Abraham, in fact, was given God's blessing before he was circumcised; his later circumcision was a "seal" given to him because of his faith in God's gift. Paul recalls the quaint accounts of Abraham and Sarah's experience told in Genesis 17 and 18 (see Rom 4:19). When God appears to Abraham and promises him he will be the "father of many nations" (Gen 17:4 AT) and furthermore that his wife Sarah would conceive a son, Abraham "fell on his face and laughed. He said to himself, Can a 100-year-old man become a father, or Sarah, a 90-year-old woman, have a child?" (Gen 17:17). This preposterous prediction is repeated in the next chapter of Genesis when three mysterious visitors come to the tent of Abraham and Sarah at Mamre. There, too, the visitor predicts that in due season Sarah will have conceived a son. This time it is Sarah's turn to laugh: "I'm no longer able to have children and my husband's old" (Gen 18:12).

In effect, the barrenness of Abraham and Sarah is a "weakness" equivalent to that of the Crucified Jesus; but, as the visitor to Abraham's tent declares, "Is anything too difficult for the LORD?" (Gen 18:14). Paul realizes that the same God who gave life to the barren womb of Sarah is the God of Israel who works in the world through the "weakness" of the Crucified Christ. In Romans 4, Paul describes God as one "who gives life to the dead," who "calls things that don't exist into existence," who "makes the ungodly righteous" (Rom 4:17, 5). The passage comes to a close by making explicit the connection between God's transformation of the "weakness" of Abraham and Sarah and that of the Crucified Christ: "But the scripture that says *it was credited to him* wasn't written only for Abraham's sake. It was written also for our sake, because it is going to be credited to us too. It will be credited to those of us who have faith in the one who raised Jesus our Lord from the dead. He was handed over because of our mistakes, and he was raised to meet the requirements of righteousness for us" (Rom 4:23-25).

Paul goes further and finds in his own experience—his "weakness"—a confirmation of God's power paradoxically revealed in what would be judged weakness and defeat by ordinary human standards.[12] A prime example is found in 2 Corinthians 4:7-12 where Paul speaks eloquently of his mission to proclaim the gospel as a "treasure" contained in "earthen vessels":

> But we have this treasure in clay pots so that the awesome power belongs to God and doesn't come from us. We are experiencing all kinds of trouble, but we aren't crushed. We are confused, but we aren't depressed. We are harassed, but we aren't abandoned. We are knocked down, but we aren't knocked out.
>
> We always carry Jesus' death around in our bodies so that Jesus' life can also be seen in our bodies. We who are alive are always being handed over to death for Jesus' sake so that Jesus' life can also be seen in our bodies that are dying. So death is at work in us, but life is at work in you.

The accumulation of sufferings—"weaknesses"—is considerable: afflicted, driven to despair, persecuted, struck down. Paul's lament here echoes the long litany of apostolic sufferings that he recites in 2 Corinthians 11:22-33. This list establishes his own apostolic credentials compared with the "super-apostles" (11:5) but also confirms that the God of the Crucified Christ is able to reveal divine power in human weakness. Yet even as Paul laments these sufferings he also testifies that, through the power of God, such weaknesses are transformed: he is afflicted but not crushed, perplexed but not despairing, persecuted but not forsaken, struck down but not destroyed. As with his Crucified Master, Paul carries in his "body," where his weakness is visible and on display, the "death of Jesus," but through the power of his apostolic ministry and its impact, so, too, "that Jesus' life can also be seen in our bodies" (2 Cor 4:11).

Thus Paul's own personal and apostolic experience becomes in effect a compelling revelation of the very God who works through a Crucified Messiah and raises him from the dead. Paul bears in his body both the dying and the rising of Christ. Paul speaks of this in very physical terms, not only in the listing of the physical and psychological hardships endured in the course of

---

12. Paul will frequently cite his apostolic sufferings as evidence both of his own weakness and of God's power working through it. See, e.g., Gal 6:11-18; Phil 3:2-11; 2 Cor 11:22-33; 13:1-4.

his mission, but even the "marks" on his body (see Gal 6:17), which might well be the scars left through the floggings Paul had endured (2 Cor 11:23-25), are "the marks of Jesus." Paul also speaks candidly of the less-than-overwhelming personal impact he has made on his communities and finds there further confirmation that the God of Jesus Christ Crucified is also working through Paul himself (see, e.g., 1 Cor 10:1-6, 10). Paul seems to contend that he might have avoided some of this suffering by compromising and agreeing to have his converts circumcised, as his opponents were apparently demanding (see Gal 6:12). But in doing so Paul fears that he would be hiding his allegiance to Christ in order to avoid persecution.[13] Instead, he declares, "But as for me, God forbid that I should boast about anything except for the cross of our Lord Jesus Christ. The world has been crucified to me through him, and I have been crucified to the world" (Gal 6:14).

The God revealed through the Crucified Christ is not simply one who confounds human wisdom but more importantly a God who is all-embracing and a God of extraordinary compassion and love. One of Paul's most forceful expressions of this conviction is found in Romans 5:1-11, immediately following his reflection on Abraham cited earlier.

Paul states that "the love of God has been poured out in our hearts through the Holy Spirit, who has been given to us" (Rom 5:5) and then goes on to reflect on the utter gift that is God's love: "While we were still weak, at the right moment, Christ died for ungodly people. It isn't often that someone will die for a righteous person, though maybe someone might dare to die for a good person. But God shows his love for us, because while we were still sinners Christ died for us" (5:6-8).

Here we stand at the center of Paul's understanding of the mission of Jesus and its revelation of who God is for us. The death of Jesus is "for us"—it is an act of self-giving, an act of love, on our behalf. Paul makes this clear at several places in his letters.[14] The death of Jesus on the cross reveals God's extraordinary love for us who as sinners did not deserve that love. Put another way, Paul declares that Christ died for the "ungodly" on behalf of the "God who makes the ungodly righteous" (Rom 4:5). As Charles Cousar has observed, "Behind the self-giving of Christ is the self-giving of God."[15]

Not only does the death of Jesus as an act of self-transcending love reveal God's extraordinary love for us as sinners but God's love is also revealed as all-

---

13. On the avoidance of circumcision in order to escape persecution, see de Boer, "Cross and Cosmos in Galatians," in Downs and Skinner, *The Unrelenting God*, 208–25, esp. 212–13.

14. See, e.g., Gal 1:4; 2:20; Rom 8:31-39.

15. Cousar, *A Theology of the Cross*, 26.

embracing and inclusive, extending to the vulnerable and the despised. The "God who makes the ungodly righteous" (Rom 4:5), the God "who gives life to the dead" and "calls into existence things that do not exist" (Rom 4:17) is a God whose loves reaches all nations. Paul asks, "Or is God the God of Jews only? Isn't God the God of Gentiles also? Yes, God is also the God of Gentiles. Since God is one, then the one who makes the circumcised righteous by faith will also make the one who isn't circumcised righteous through faith" (Rom 3:29-30).

The God revealed through the Crucified Christ is a reconciling God who breaks down the barriers of division—"neither Jew nor Greek; there is neither slave nor free; nor is there male and female, for you are all one in Christ Jesus" (Gal 3:28). The God of Jesus reconciles us with himself—those who had been trapped in sin and death, those separated and alienated, those far off—these are now reconciled with God not because of their own initiative but through the healing love of the God revealed through Jesus. Jesus' act of self-transcending love in dying on the cross becomes the supreme revelation of who God is for us.[16] Paul declares this in a way that also gives the ultimate meaning to his own ministry, which would take him to the Gentiles, to the people "far off":

> So then, if anyone is in Christ, that person is part of the new creation. The old things have gone away, and look, new things have arrived!
>
> All of these new things are from God, who reconciled us to himself through Christ and who gave us the ministry of reconciliation. In other words, God was reconciling the world to himself through Christ, by not counting people's sins against them. He has trusted us with this message of reconciliation.
>
> So we are ambassadors who represent Christ. God is negotiating with you through us. We beg you as Christ's representatives, "Be reconciled to God!" God caused the one who didn't know sin to be sin for our sake so that through him we could become the righteousness of God. (2 Cor 5:17-21)

Paul's new awareness of who God is through the wisdom of the cross was not a rejection of the God Paul had come to know through the scriptures and his Jewish faith but a deeper discovery. The God who forged Jewish slaves into a people and gave them a land; the God who cares for the "the immigrants, the orphans, and the widows who are among you" (Deut 16:11); the God who hears the cries of the poor; the God who brought Israel home from exile was the same God who now spoke through the Messiah, the Crucified Jesus.

---

16. In this way, Paul's fundamental conviction is very similar to that of John's theology and finds further echoes in the meaning of Jesus' death portrayed in the Synoptic Gospels. See earlier, pp. 29–77.

Seen through the lens of Jesus' death on the cross, the infinitely tender and awesomely transcendent God of Israel was clearly the God of all—Jew and Gentile—and a God whose compassion for the most vulnerable and despised could not be denied.

III. Jesus, Crucified and Risen, Is the New Adam

For Paul, Jesus is a representative human being whose death and resurrection save humanity from the power of sin and death. Jesus is the dominant presence in all of Paul's writings but, unlike the Gospels, Paul only refers in passing to the details of Jesus' life and death.[17] Like a laser beam, Paul's attention is focused on the central reality of Jesus' life and mission—namely his death and resurrection. Paul cites the creedal formula of 1 Corinthians 15:3-4, a vital part of the Christian tradition in which he had been formed, that has the same focus: "I passed on to you as most important what I also received: Christ died for our sins in line with the scriptures, he was buried, and he rose on the third day in line with the scriptures." Even though Paul refrains from narrating details of Jesus' life, the apostle's multiple references to Jesus' death on the cross bind the figure of Christ to a time and place and firmly root him in human history.[18]

For Paul, Jesus was, in effect, the representative human being. In him all of humanity's fate stood in the balance. Jesus was the "new Adam" whose righteousness before God would reverse the condemnation humanity faced because of the scourge of sin unleashed in the world through the sin of the first Adam (see Paul's extended reflection in Rom 5:12-21). Jesus was the "first of many brothers and sisters" (Rom 8:29) in whose image all of those called by God would be conformed. In the death and resurrection of Jesus, all humanity was now capable of defeating death and was being offered the possibility of new life. As Paul states, "The love of Christ controls us, because we have concluded this: one died for the sake of all; therefore, all died. He died for the sake of all so that those who are alive should live not for themselves but for the one who died for them and was raised" (2 Cor 5:14-15). Jesus, dead and risen, was the catalyst for the "new creation": "The old things have gone away, and look, new things have arrived!" (2 Cor 5:17; see also Gal 6:1).

---

17. However, Paul is well aware of the basic facts of Jesus' crucifixion; on this see Allison, *Constructing Jesus*, 392–403.

18. On this see Schnelle, *Apostle Paul*, 430–23. The cross remains the fundamental refutation of Docetism and Gnosticism.

A key to Paul's thought is his understanding of "sin."[19] By "sin" Paul does not refer primarily to individual immoral acts but to a quasi-cosmic force that entered the world with Adam's sin and through the accumulative power of evil, reigns over the world, holding humanity in its grip and condemning human beings to death. "So, in the same way that sin entered the world through one person, and death came through sin, so death spread to all human beings with the result that all sinned" (Rom 5:12). The power of sin thwarts the attempts of human beings to do good, whether as Jews prompted to do so by observance of the Law from Moses or as Gentiles attempting to discern the will of God through observance of nature.[20] In the famous soliloquy of Romans 7, Paul—speaking as it were on behalf of all humanity—laments, "I don't know what I'm doing, because I don't do what I want to do. Instead, I do the thing that I hate" (7:15; see the entire passage, Rom 7:14-25). This is what Paul means by living "according to the flesh" rather than "according to the Spirit" (AT; see Rom 8:1-17). The human inclination to be self-seeking at the expense of others; to allow our baser instincts to rule us; to abuse our bodies through excess and lack of self-discipline; to give into factions and quarreling; to ignore the needs of others, especially the poor—these are the things Paul confronts his communities about in all his letters.[21] This vicious power of sin that traps humanity and thwarts its best intentions leads ultimately to death itself. For Paul, death is the "last enemy" (1 Cor 15:26).

Paul is convinced that through his death on the cross—an act of consummate love—and through his resurrection from the dead Jesus Christ radically breaks this deadly power of sin and paves the way for those who believe in Jesus to be able to experience freedom from death and to enjoy abundant new life with God. But how does this happen? Here is where Paul himself—and subsequent Christian tradition—wrestles with a variety of explanations. Paul admits that his explanations are of limited value—after all he is trying to plumb the depths of God's mysterious being. As he exclaims in trying to fathom the destiny of Israel, "God's riches, wisdom, and knowledge are so deep! They are as mysterious as his judgments, and they are as hard to track as his paths!" (Rom 11:33). Nevertheless, for the sake of the communities to whom he writes, Paul attempts to explain the saving power of Jesus' death on the cross by turning to biblical traditions and known human transactions that also involve an exchange or a remission of a debt or in some way lead to

---

19. On Paul's notion of "sin," see Dunn, *The Theology of Paul the Apostle*, 111–24.

20. Paul argues to this conclusion in the opening chapters of Romans. While the Jews had the advantage of the Law from Moses, they, too, fall short of righteousness. As Paul concludes: "Both Jews and Greeks are under the power of sin" (Rom 3:9).

21. See Paul's list of the "works of the flesh" in Gal 5:19-21 (AT).

expiation of sin. Each metaphor Paul will use throws some light on the meaning of Jesus' death on the cross but each is also limited and cannot be pressed as a complete explanation.[22]

In 2 Corinthians, for example, Paul uses a variety of metaphors in rapid succession to affirm that the death of Jesus saves us from the power of sin. Jesus' died "for the sake of all" (2 Cor 5:14-15), the preposition *hyper* evoking the notion of sacrifice. Jesus gives his life on behalf of us; through the death of Jesus, God reconciles himself with humanity (2 Cor 5:18-19), implying that a primal alienation of humans from God through sin is now dissolved. Indeed, God made Jesus to be "sin" so that we might become justified with God (2 Cor 5:21), implying that Jesus bears the sins of all humanity and substitutes for human guilt, reminiscent of the role of the scapegoat upon whom the sins of Israel were laden.[23] Paul reflects in a similar way in Galatians 3:13 where he speaks of Christ becoming a "curse" for us. Here Paul draws on Deuteronomy 21:23 (AT), which declares that "God's curse is on those who are hung on a tree."[24] In dying on the cross Jesus takes upon himself the curse that we who are sinners would have earned.

In virtually all of these and the other metaphors Paul uses, there is the underlying conviction that through his death on the cross, Jesus—God's Messiah and the one in whom all humanity's fate stands—substitutes for us and absorbs the punishment for sin that all of us deserved and should have experienced. In subsequent Christian tradition, this would lead to various theologies of "atonement."[25] At its core, the notion of atonement attempts to express what Paul asserts: namely, that in dying on the cross Jesus takes our place and through his dying and rising "atones" or "satisfies" the punishment

---

22. Charles Cousar's comment is very helpful here:

> Nevertheless, Paul's language, like the language of the Synoptics, is metaphorical and indirect. He speaks about the unspeakable and confesses that God and God's ways transcend his own capacity to describe and proclaim them in human language....Nowhere is this more evident than in Paul's soteriological language, about what God did in regard to human sin, about why Christ died. Paul employs a whole host of images, some drawn from the Scriptures, some from the early Christian tradition, some from the common language of the day, to express what is ultimately unexpressable. The powerful and mysterious significance of Jesus' death is articulated carefully but indirectly in terms of what is known (setting relationships right, reconciling alienated people, not keeping a record of the trespasses of the guilty, expiating for sins, paying debts, triumphing over enemies, liberating the enslaved, etc.). (*A Theology of the Cross*, 84–85)

See also Carroll and Green, *The Death of Jesus in Early Christianity*, 125.

23. See the extensive discussion of Christ's death as a sacrifice in Paul's theology in Dunn, *The Theology of Paul the Apostle*, 207–33.

24. See previously, p. 5.

25. On atonement theology, see Hengel, *The Atonement*; Eberhart, *The Sacrifice of Jesus*; Finlan, *Problems with Atonement*.

that our innate sinfulness requires. The problem with many expressions of atonement theology is that they attempt to fill out the scenario implied in such substitution language and extend the implications to God's own role.[26] It is God's wrath at human sinfulness that must be appeased through Jesus' death; God's "honor" must be recognized through the sacrifice of a fitting victim; it is the cost of sin that must be paid to God by the death of Jesus in order to ransom humanity from death. Atonement thus understood becomes "penal substitution." The image of God that can emerge from such forms of atonement theology is that of an arbitrary and cruel despot who demands the terrible price of his own son's death in order to be appeased. This has led to an often heated debate, particularly in Protestant circles, triggered by those who insist on the centrality of penal substitutionary atonement as the most appropriate way to understand the salvific meaning of Jesus' death on the cross.[27]

But Paul's metaphors are meant to be analogies in which only one or more dimensions of the metaphor are apt for throwing some light on the mystery of the cross but are essentially limited in their scope. As the scholastics knew well, when attempting to describe God, only the one dimension fits and all the rest do not. God, for example, may be compared to a human father or parent, as the scriptures do, in that God is loving and faithful to us, but in every other way God is *not* like us or any human parent. God is totally other. So, too, the metaphors of substitution that Paul uses to describe the redeeming power of Jesus' death on the cross aptly describe the liberating effect of Jesus' death and resurrection but these same metaphors become distorted when we fill out the scenario and describe God's role in their light.

What is clear in Paul's theology—and what should temper every expression of atonement theology—is that Paul affirms that through the cross of Christ God's redeeming love for the world—not God's wrath—is proclaimed. As Paul tells the Thessalonians, "God didn't intend for us to suffer his wrath but rather to possess salvation through our Lord Jesus Christ. Jesus died for us so that, whether we are awake or asleep, we will live together with him" (1 Thess 5:9-10). The driving force of God's love is expressly stated by Paul in the key text of Romans 5:8—"But God shows his love for us, because while we were still sinners Christ died for us." And the same conviction rises to its most eloquent expression in the conclusion of Romans 8 where Paul reflects on human destiny: "I'm convinced that nothing can separate us from God's

---

26. See Finlan, *Problems with Atonement*, 43–44.

27. On this see Baker and Green, *Recovering the Scandal of the Cross*; McKnight, *A Community Called Atonement*; Travis, *Christ and the Judgment of God*.

love in Christ Jesus our Lord: not death or life, not angels or rulers, not present things or future things, not powers or height or depth, or any other thing that is created" (Rom 8:38-39). In Philippians when Paul makes an appeal for mutual love and harmony within the community, he cites the hymn that tracks the "descent" of Christ from his existence in the "form of God" (Phil 2:6) and becoming human in order that through his obedience and his death on the cross Christ can reveal God's glory to the world (Phil 2:6-11). The implication is clear—the Philippians are to "adopt the attitude that was in Christ Jesus"—namely, that through Jesus' death on the cross, an act of self-transcending love, the very mind of God is manifested and becomes the norm of human behavior among those who believe (2:5).

IV. Life in the Spirit Begins with Baptism

Through baptism the Christian shares in the saving power of Christ's death and resurrection and is thereby enabled to live a life imbued with the Spirit of God, a life that characterizes not only the individual believer but also the church itself. Paul is convinced that in baptism the one who believes in Jesus shares in the death and resurrection of Christ and is made a new creation, a new human being. Baptism and the newness of life it engenders in the Christian is the proving ground of Christ's redemptive work. Paul reflects on this in Romans 6:

> Or don't you know that all who were baptized into Christ Jesus were baptized into his death? Therefore, we were buried together with him through baptism into his death, so that just as Christ was raised from the dead through the glory of the Father, we too can walk in newness of life. If we were united together in a death like his, we will also be united together in a resurrection like his. This is what we know: the person that we used to be was crucified with him in order to get rid of the corpse that had been controlled by sin. That way we wouldn't be slaves to sin anymore, because a person who has died has been freed from sin's power. But if we died with Christ, we have faith that we will also live with him. We know that Christ has been raised from the dead and he will never die again. Death no longer has power over him. He died to sin once and for all with this death, but he lives for God with his life. In the same way, you also should consider yourselves dead to sin but alive for God in Christ Jesus. (Rom 6:3-11)

Paul portrays human behavior as either dominated by the flesh—which Paul characterizes as self-centered and self-indulgent—or a life dominated by the Spirit that is manifested in goodness, generosity, and self-transcending love.[28] The person who lives by the spirit is "in Christ"; that is, so transformed by the power of Christ's death and resurrection that one identifies heart and soul with Christ and his mode of being. Being "in Christ" ultimately means that the believer will experience Christ's own destiny with God. This is the beautiful vision of Christian life and destiny that Paul expresses in Romans 8:

> All who are led by God's Spirit are God's sons and daughters. You didn't receive a spirit of slavery to lead you back again into fear, but you received a Spirit that shows you are adopted as children. With this Spirit, we cry, "Abba, Father." The same Spirit agrees with our spirit, that we are God's children. But if we are children, we are also heirs. We are God's heirs and fellow heirs with Christ, if we really suffer with him so that we can also be glorified with him. (Rom 8:14-17)

For Paul the death and resurrection of Jesus empower the Christian to live the life of the Spirit, enabling the baptized to move from a life trapped in sin or in the "flesh" (AT) to a new life animated by God's own Spirit and now capable of virtue. Thus for Paul this new state of life does not come about by striving to lead a virtuous life; instead, the new state of life comes first through God's grace, and a virtuous life is its manifestation. This is often referred to as moving "from the indicative to the imperative" rather than "from the imperative to the indicative." Paul's moral exhortations persuade the Christian to live in accord with the transformed being they now are. Paul's ethical vision is summed up in a quotation attributed to the ancient Greek poet Pindar: "Become who you are."

What is true of the individual Christian is also true of the Christian community itself. The relationships among the Christians are to be characterized by those virtues that he lists as the "fruit of the Spirit" and therefore characterized by mutual love, forbearance, gracious speech, forgiveness, and care for the weak and the vulnerable.[29] Paul is particularly distressed by factionalism, which appears on his list of "works of the flesh" (see Gal 5:20 AT) and is confronted in his opening exhortations to the communities at Corinth

---

28. Paul spells out these contrasting modes of living in several places in his letters; see in particular Gal 5:16-26 (AT). The "works of the flesh" are "fornication, impurity, licentiousness, idolatry, sorcery, enmities, strife, jealously, anger, quarrels, dissensions, factions, envy, drunkenness, carousing, and things like these". In contrast the "fruit of the Spirit" is "love, joy, peace, patience, kindness, generosity, faithfulness, gentleness, and self-control."

29. See, e.g., Gal 5:22-23; 2 Cor 6:6-7; 8:7; Phil 4:8-9.

93

and Philippi.[30] Paul's conviction that such divisions are incompatible with the example of Jesus is especially clear in the later chapters of 1 Corinthians. After dealing with a host of pastoral problems in the main body of the letter, Paul turns to an issue that is particularly painful. In the manner in which they are conducting the celebration of the Lord's Supper, the wealthier members of the community are embarrassing the poor members by bringing more lavish food in contrast with the meager rations of the poor members. In a telling move, Paul appeals to the example of Jesus at the Last Supper. On the eve of his death on the cross, Jesus had shared with his disciples the bread now declared to be his body, "which is for you," and the cup of wine, which was now "the new covenant in my blood." Thus the authentic celebration of the Lord's Supper is to be characterized by a bond of love in which there is no factionalism and all are respected and cared for and so becomes a living remembrance of the very nature and purpose of Jesus' own death on the cross (see 1 Cor 11:17-34).

Responding to this pastoral problem no doubt motivates what Paul speaks of next in his description of what the community is to be—a community in which there is a variety of gifts expressive of the one spirit (1 Cor 12:1-11), a community that is in effect the "body of Christ" where all the members work together and where the most vulnerable members are the most honored (1 Cor 12:12-31), and, finally, a community that understands and exemplifies that the greatest gift is love (1 Cor 13:1-13).

There is little doubt that Paul's vision of such a community is prompted by his contemplation of Jesus Crucified who "loved me and gave himself for me" (Gal 2:20). Consistently Paul appeals to the image of the cross of Jesus as the countercultural standard of living in integrity, self-giving, care for the vulnerable, and mutual love that stands over against the patterns of the "flesh" that ignore and despise such virtues.[31]

Conclusion

For Paul the apostle, the death of Jesus on the cross—and its ultimate outcome in resurrection—was the supreme expression of the messianic mission of Jesus and the pattern for human destiny itself. Paul insists that he arrived at this core conviction through God's own revelation to him. Paul, a firebrand persecutor of the early followers of Jesus and zealous for his own

---

30. 1 Cor 1:10-17; Phil 2:1-4.

31. On this see Finney, *Honour and Conflict in the Ancient World*, esp. 88–91. See also N. Elliott, "The Anti-Imperial Message of the Cross," in Horsley, *Paul and Empire: Religion and Power in Roman Imperial Society*, 167.

Jewish heritage, was transformed by his encounter with the Crucified and Risen Christ. From then on he had to reconsider everything he believed and discover anew the God of Israel and the startling and radical nature of God's way of working in human history. Through the cross of Jesus, God revealed an intense, freely given, and inclusive love for the world, a love that would rescue humanity from the power of sin and death. Based on that conviction Paul felt compelled to bring the gospel of God's redeeming love to the Gentiles, and from that same conviction he would develop his insights into what it meant to live a life "in Christ" and to be a community that bore the name of Christ.

Chapter Five

The Saving Death of Jesus in Other New Testament Traditions

The conviction of the four gospels and of Paul that the death of Jesus on the cross saves humanity from sin is also firmly confessed in other New Testament texts. We now turn to some of these texts where the meaning of Jesus' death on the cross is an explicit and characteristic focus.

I. Colossians and Ephesians: The Cross of Christ and the Reconciliation of the World

Paul himself describes one of the consequences of the death of Jesus as "reconciliation." As an act of self-transcending love, the death of Jesus—God's Son and Messiah—breaks the bonds of death and sin that held humanity captive and alienates them from God. Through baptism those who believe in Jesus experience liberation from death and the promise of new life in Christ, becoming a "new creation" (see 2 Cor 5:17-21).

This motif of reconciliation is amplified in the Letters to the Colossians and Ephesians. A majority of modern scholars consider these two letters

97

to be deuteropauline texts based on differences in literary style and some theological perspectives that distinguish them from the so-called authentic Pauline Letters.[1] However, both letters have close affinity with Paul's thought and both describe the impact of the death of Jesus as effecting reconciliation, although each letter gives this motif a different emphasis. We cannot be certain of the sequence of the two letters, but most interpreters see Colossians as earlier than Ephesians and even having influenced the author of Ephesians.[2]

The Letter to the Colossians: The Reconciliation of the Universe

"Paul," the claimed author of the letter, writes to a community in western Asia Minor that he has not visited or evangelized.[3] There are problems facing the community caused by some who are promoting a strange set of teachings, ritual practices, and ascetical demands (see, e.g., Col 2:16-23). Unlike Paul's opponents in Galatians and 2 Corinthians, these do not seem to be "Judaizers" who are questioning Paul's message about justification apart from observance of the Mosaic Law, but appear to represent some form of syncretism.[4] The basic threat is that these false teachers stoke the fear that the salvation proclaimed by Paul and his associates is not adequate to counter the threats posed by alien beings within the universe who have the power to control human destiny. The response of the letter is to strongly affirm that through the saving power of his death on the cross, the universal lordship of Christ extends over the entire universe.

Explicit references to the "cross" of Christ occur in two key passages of Colossians, 1:15-20 and 2:12-15.

Colossians 1:15-20: Making Peace through the Blood of His Cross

This famous passage probably originated as an early Christian hymn that was adapted by the author of Colossians and made a linchpin of the entire letter. It is one of the New Testament's most profound expressions of Christian faith in the divinity of Christ and the universal scope of his redemptive work.

The passage begins by describing Christ as "the image of the invisible God" and the "first over all creation" (Col 1:15; literally the text states that Christ is the "first born" [*prōtotokos*] of all creation). There is no doubt that

---

1. See the discussion in Roetzel, *The Letters of Paul*, esp. 133–60.

2. See MacDonald, *Colossians, Ephesians*, esp. 4–6.

3. See the discussion of authorship in Best, *Ephesians*, 7–20. We will use "Paul" as name of the author although this is not certain.

4. See Perkins, *Ephesians*, 27–32; Best, *Ephesians*, 63–75.

Jewish wisdom motifs have a strong influence on content of this hymn; "Wisdom" is proclaimed in the Old Testament as the very "image" or revelation of God; "wisdom" is, in a sense, the metaphorical personification of God.[5] Early Jewish Christian reflection on Jesus as the revealer of God drew on this biblical tradition, as evident in the prologue of John's Gospel.[6] Likewise, "wisdom" was declared to be the pattern of creation itself—ensuring that the universe reflects the beauty and power of the God who created it.[7] The description of Christ as "first over all creation" is a more explicitly Christian motif (see also 1:18, "firstborn from among the dead"); Paul likewise speaks of the Risen Christ as the "first" of many generations (Rom 8:29).

The reference to creation leads into a strong emphasis on Jesus as the very instrument through which the world was created and sets up the fundamental argument of the letter that counters the fear of alien powers present in the universe and harmful to human beings, a view apparently promoted by the opponents. In Christ,

> all things were created by him:
>> both in the heavens and on the earth,
>> the things that are visible and the things that are invisible.
>>> Whether they are thrones or powers,
>>> or rulers or authorities,
>> all things were created through him and for him.
>
> He existed before all things,
>> and all things are held together in him. (Col 1:16-17)

At this stage in the letter, these created beings are not labeled as hostile or threatening; as part of creation through Christ they are assumed to be good. Yet later in the letter the author says that Christ "disarmed" the "rulers and authorities" and "exposed them to public disgrace by leading them in a triumphal parade" (2:15). As noted earlier, it is probable that the opponents themselves raised the specter of supernatural beings or forces in the universe who held power over human destiny and were to be feared (see, e.g., Col 2:8, 20).

Christ is also acclaimed as "the head of the body, the church" (Col 1:18;

---

5. See for example, Prov 1:20-30; 8–9; Sir 24; Wis 8:22-30; Bar 3:9-37.

6. See the discussion on the influence of wisdom on New Testament Christology in Dunn, *The Theology of Paul*, 267–81.

7. Paul draws on this tradition in Rom 1:18-25.

see also 1:24). Paul described the church as the "body of Christ" in the famous passage of 1 Corinthians 12:12-31 but did not refer to Christ as the "head" of the body. Paul uses the image of the body and its many members to emphasize the unity of the church and the complementarity of its members' gifts (see also 1 Cor 12:4-11). Here, however, the author of Colossians wants to emphasize the exaltation of Christ above every created being and the extension of his redemptive power to all reality. Christ has "the first place in everything" and, in what is a supreme expression of Christian faith, "all the fullness of God was pleased to live in him" (Col 1:18-19).

This leads directly into the climatic verse of the hymn and Colossian's affirmation of the reconciling power of Jesus' death on the cross: "And he [God] reconciled all things to himself through him—whether things on earth or in the heavens. He brought peace through the blood of his cross" (1:20).[8] The reconciliation in view is not simply between Gentile and Jew as Ephesians will emphasize,[9] nor even simply reconciliation between God and humans as Paul acclaims in 2 Corinthians 5:17-21, but the reconciliation of the entire universe. The cosmic status of Christ as "before all things" and as the one in whom "all things are held together" and as the "head of the body, the church" ensures the cosmic and universal scope of Jesus' redemptive death. Neither sin or death or any other power can make null the impact of Jesus' reconciling work (Col 1:17-18).

Paul had this same expansive intuition in his ecstatic reflection found in Romans 8: "Who will separate us from Christ's love? Will we be separated by trouble, or distress, or harassment, or famine, or nakedness, or danger, or sword? . . . I'm convinced that nothing can separate us from God's love in Christ Jesus our Lord: not death or life, not angels or rulers, not present things or future things, not powers or height or depth, or any other thing that is created" (8:35, 38-39). Also like Paul, the author of Colossians emphasizes that the initiative and source for the world's reconciliation is the love of God revealed in the self-transcending death of Jesus on the cross (1:20). As we have seen consistently in the Pauline tradition, there is no scenario where Jesus dies to assuage divine wrath or is offered as some sort of payment or ransom to satisfy God's requirements for making peace. On the contrary, the initiative to reconcile humanity to God and indeed to reconcile the entire universe comes from God's own love manifested in the cross of Christ.

8. The vivid phrase, "the blood of his cross" is unique to Colossians and is not found in the Pauline literature.

9. See below, pp. 102–7.

Colossians 2:12-15: The Triumph of the Cross

The second key text in Colossians begins by restating a fundamental Pauline conviction: through baptism the believer is immersed in the paschal mystery of Christ's own dying and rising: "You were buried with him through baptism and raised with him through faith in the power of God, who raised him from the dead" (2:12). This thought is stated in other terms in the following verse: "When you were dead because of the things you had done wrong and because your body wasn't circumcised [literally, "the uncircumcision of your flesh"], God made you alive with Christ and forgave all the things you had done wrong" (2:13). The phrase "uncircumcision of your flesh" implies that the audience addressed here is mainly Gentile—similar to Ephesians 2:11-12, which speaks of the addressees as ones "called 'uncircumcised' by Jews who are physically circumcised."[10] Their plight as Gentiles meant they were "dead" because of sin and not included in the ranks of God's own people. But the focus of Colossians is not on the division between Gentile and Jew but on the overall vulnerability of those who in their past had not yet experienced deliverance from fear and hopelessness. But now through the cross of Christ, God "made you alive together with Christ and forgave us all the things you had done wrong" (Col 2:13).

The segment concludes with a dramatic and unique reference to the saving impact of Jesus' death on the cross (Col 2:14-15): "He destroyed the record of the debt we owed, with its requirements that worked against us. He canceled it by nailing it to the cross. When he disarmed the rulers and authorities, he exposed them to public disgrace by leading them in a triumphal parade."

It is not clear in the text whether the subject "he" remains "God" or has now switched to "Christ."[11] In either case, the sense of the text is that God is working through the death and resurrection of Jesus. A new metaphorical element describes the fate of those trapped in sin as having a legal record or document that records the plight of sinful humanity—a writ of condemnation apparently originating from the "rulers and authorities" who threaten humanity.[12] Speaking of this written "record" or bond "with its legal demands" might imply the obligations of the Jewish law (which Paul wrestles with in

---

10. See below, p. 104.

11. See Dunn, *The Epistles to the Colossians and to Philemon*, 167, who concludes that it is more appropriate that the subject be Christ; likewise, Wilson, *Colossians and Philemon*, 211.

12. The Greek term *cheirographon* is found only here in the New Testament and means literally a "handwritten document" and in Greco-Roman literature refers to a "certificate of indebtedness," an "account," or a "record of debts"; see Danker, ed., *A Greek-English Lexicon of the New Testament and Other Early Christian Literature*, 1083.

Rom 7:14-25), but the term for "law" (*nomos*) is not used here. Instead the reference may have a more generic meaning: the Colossians in their former state were held accountable to the threats and condemnations of the alien powers, the "rulers and authorities." But now through the reconciling death of Christ that decree of condemnation and the fear and despair it represented have been "set aside" and "nailed to the cross." Surely this is an allusion to the custom of placing on the cross of a condemned criminal a placard naming his crimes.[13] The author dramatically reverses this decree of condemnation: instead of sealing the public shame and misery of the one crucified, now God's power in Christ makes this placard nailed to the cross of Christ a sign of victory.

The final verse of this passage makes precisely this point. Like a triumphant emperor returning from battle and displaying his captives and booty for all to see, so God disarms the powerful beings who had been a threat, "he exposed them to public disgrace by leading them in a triumphal parade" (2:15). The Greek word for "disarms"—*apekdysamenos*—literally means to take off a garment or to strip; thus the sense is that God exposes the impotence of these supposed powers and makes an example of them. Before the almighty power of God and the transforming power of Christ's death and resurrection, such supposed powers pose no threat at all for those who believe in Christ.[14]

The Letter to the Ephesians: Breaking Down the Dividing Wall and Building the New Temple

There is much unresolved debate about the origin and purpose of Ephesians.[15] In general the author appears to address a community or communities that are composed of both Jews and Gentiles. We cannot be certain of the specific context of the letter's audience but there is no sense of any strong conflict between the followers of Jesus and rival Jewish leaders, as found for example in Matthew's Gospel. Neither is the question of the legitimacy of the mission to the Gentiles in play; it seems that this was no longer a problem for the author and his audience, as it still was for Paul. At the outset of the letter, the author refers to "we" as sharing in the common fate of humanity prior

13. See earlier, p. 3.

14. See the comment of Wilson, *Colossians and Philemon*: "Our author hammers home his message, that in Christ they already have all that is required: they are fulfilled in him who is the head of all rule and dominion" (214).

15. See the extensive discussion in Best, *Ephesians*, 36–46. He speculates that Ephesians may have emerged from a quasi–"Pauline school" and its authors write in the manner of Pauline theology to the community addressed.

to the salvation brought by Christ and speaks in generic terms about having lived in the world doing "whatever felt good" and being "children headed for punishment just like everyone else" (2:3).

Echoing the Pauline conviction of Romans 5:6-11, the author emphasizes that salvation came not through any human merit but from the promptings of God's own great love: "However, God is rich in mercy. He brought us to life with Christ while we were dead as a result of those things that we did wrong. He did this because of the great love that he has for us. You are saved by God's grace! And God raised us up and seated us in the heavens with Christ Jesus" (Eph 2:4-6).[16] This transformation, which is prompted by God's love, is effected through the death and resurrection of Jesus: "We have been ransomed through his Son's blood, and we have forgiveness for our failures based on his overflowing grace, which he poured over us with wisdom and understanding" (Eph 1:7-8) Later in the letter, when urging the community to "be kind, compassionate, and forgiving to each other, in the same way God forgave you in Christ," the author also uses sacrificial imagery to describe the love of God that reaches us through the death of Jesus: "Therefore, imitate God like dearly loved children. Live your life with love, following the example of Christ, who loved us and gave himself for us. He was a sacrificial offering that smelled sweet to God" (Eph 4:32; 5:1-2).

Although the notion of the death of Jesus as effecting reconciliation is a motif already found in Paul's letters (see, e.g., Rom 5:10-11; 2 Cor 5:18-21), it takes on a new tone and emphasis in a beautiful key passage of Ephesians 2:11-22. The generic reference to the need for salvation becomes specific to the status of Gentiles and Jews beginning with 2:11. The author speaks specifically of "you Gentiles by physical descent" and those "called 'uncircumcised' by Jews who are physically circumcised" and will use this cultural and religious division as the starting point for reflecting on the death of Jesus as an act of universal reconciliation.[17]

The passage can be divided into three segments. The first, 2:11-12, describes the division of humanity based on the different experiences of Gentile and Jew. The second, 2:13-18, speaks of Christ's reconciling death on the cross, which breaks down the barriers of enmity. And the concluding

---

16. See previously, p. 87, in "Paul and the Saving Power of the Cross."

17. This is a contrast point with Colossians, which also describes the cosmic scope of Christ's work of reconciliation; in Ephesians the focus is on the human community and the church itself represented in the relationship of Jew and Gentile. See earlier, pp. 98–102. Note that the author by referring to "Jews who are physically circumcised" (literally "a physical circumcision made in the flesh by human hands"; Eph 2:11) seems to downplay the religious significance of circumcision, which for Israel was the sign of its covenant relationship with God; see Perkins, *Ephesians*, 67.

103

segment, 2:19-22, describes the impact of Christ's reconciling death manifested in the unity and dynamic exaltation of the church.

Ephesians 2:11-12: A World Divided

The author begins by reminding the Gentiles in his audience of their bleak past history from a religious point of view. They were "without Christ," "aliens rather than citizens of Israel," "strangers to the covenants of God's promise," with "no hope and no God" (2:12). In general this was a stock Jewish assessment of the religious plight of the Gentile world.[18] Not belonging to Israel and not having the benefit of the various covenants God made with his chosen people and immersed in idolatry, indeed the Gentiles had no reason to hope and were "atheists" (that is, "without God"—*atheoi* in Greek). But, as we will see, the author is not leading up to a conclusion that through Christ the Gentiles will now be able to become members of God's people Israel. Rather, through the cross of Christ both Gentile and Jew will become part of an entirely new community.

Ephesians 2:13-18: Breaking Down the Dividing Wall and Making Peace

Some suggest that the poetic elements of this section may have originated as an early Christian hymn, but if so it has been thoroughly integrated into the author's own discourse.[19] The opening verse of this section proclaims the reconciling effect of the death of Jesus: "But now, thanks to Christ Jesus, you who once were so far away have been brought near by the blood of Christ" (2:13). The terms "far away" and "brought near" seem to draw on Isaiah 57:19, which speaks of "utter prosperity to those far and near," a text the author will certainly refer to in Ephesians 2:17. There is some ambiguity about what people are being referred to as the "far away." In the original context of Isaiah, the most likely reference is to diaspora Jews scattered through exile. But here in Ephesians the reference must be to the Gentiles whose plight was described in 2:11. There are several places in the Old Testament where Gentiles also were described as the people "far away."[20] Through the blood of Christ the Gentiles are now "brought near"—not to Israel, as would have been the case with Gentile proselytes to Judaism, but to God from

---

18. See ibid., 69–70.

19. Suggestions that this passage incorporates a traditional hymn have focused particularly on Eph 2:14-18. See the thorough assessment in Best, *Ephesians*, 247–50, who concludes that the passage is more likely the work of the author of Ephesians.

20. See, e.g., Deut 29:22; 1 Kgs 8:41; Ps 148:14.

whom they were estranged and to a new people forged from both Jew and Gentile.

To the metaphor of "far" and "near" is joined that of the "dividing wall" (Eph 2:14 AT).[21] Here, too, there is some ambiguity about what precisely the author means by this image.[22] For some the "dividing wall" refers most probably to the barrier that divided the courtyard of the Gentiles from the interior areas of the temple complex in Jerusalem.[23] Gentiles were forbidden to come closer to the zone of the sacred for fear of defilement of the sanctuary. Others, however, doubt that this is the "the dividing wall" the author is referring to, despite its vivid appeal. The reference to the abolishment of the law in the following verse may suggest that the author has in mind the metaphorical barrier of separation that divided those who were faithful to the law from those who did not observe it. The *Letter of Aristeas*, for example, refers to God surrounding those observant of the Law "with unbroken palisades and iron walls to prevent our mixing with any of the other peoples... thus being kept pure in body and soul."[24]

In any case, whether the author has in mind the temple dividing wall or the "wall" around the Law or simply a more generic metaphorical reference, it is a barrier that signifies "hostility between us" (see Eph 2:14 AT)—namely between Jew and Gentile. Since there is no sense in other parts of the letter about current tensions or hostility between the Jewish and Gentile members of the community, it is likely that the author is using the case of the cultural, religious, and historic separation of Jew and Gentile as an example of the divisions and enmity that have been chronically present in human civilization and were even to be found within Judaism and within the Christian communities themselves. Furthermore, this alienation and mutual hostility that is symptomatic of the human condition was itself a result of humanity's alienation from God through sin. This was an affirmation of the biblical saga beginning with the story of Cain and Abel.

It is this chronic alienation, this "dividing wall" of hostility that the death of Jesus on the cross breaks down, creating in and through his sacrificial death "one new person out of the two groups, making peace. He reconciled them

---

21. The CEB translates the Greek term "dividing wall" (*mesotoixon tou phragmou*) as a "barrier of hatred," which, although not literal, picks up the sense of the word *echthra* (i.e., hostility) at the end of the verse. If the author of Ephesians is referring either to the wall dividing Jew from Gentile in the Jerusalem temple or the "fence" around the law, neither would be characterized as a "barrier of hatred" as such.

22. See list of possibilities in Barth, *Ephesians 1–3*, 283–91.

23. The sensitivity involved in crossing this barrier is illustrated in Acts 21:27-29 when Paul is accused of having brought "Greeks" (i.e., Gentiles) into the temple area.

24. Aristeas, 139; quoted in Perkins, *Ephesians*, 71–72, to support the interpretation that Paul refers here to the Mosaic Law.

both as one body to God by the cross, which ended the hostility to God" (Eph 2:15-16). Here the author of Ephesians amplifies Paul's reflections on the reconciling consequence of the death and resurrection of Jesus. The division between Jew and Gentile becomes a classic illustration of the multiple divisions that afflicted humanity because of sin. Jesus, through his self-transcending love that brought him to the cross and because of the reconciling love of God that death on the cross revealed, proclaims "peace" and offers the power of reconciliation to the world (2:17).

Ephesians 2:19-22: The Household of God

The final segment of this remarkable passage reflects on the corporate impact of the death and resurrection of Jesus. The new reconciled people formed of those who were once "far away" and those were "near," of those who were "strangers" and "aliens" and those who were already part of God's people have now been transformed into "fellow citizens" belonging "to God's household" (Eph 2:19). Where Paul's focus was on the personal transformation of the believers who are reconciled to God through the death of Jesus, the author of Ephesians considers the birth of the church as a community of reconciled people. This household [*oikeioi*] of God is "built on the foundation of the apostles and prophets" (2:20). The vantage point of the letter looks back on the generation of the founding "apostles," suggesting its date of origin later in the first century. It speaks of "prophets," which, coming after the mention of the apostles, probably refers to the early Christian prophets who had a significant teaching role in the community (see also Eph 3:5; 4:11). Christ Jesus himself is the "cornerstone" of the entire edifice; the term *akrogōniaios* could mean either the "foundation" stone upon which the edifice is built or the "keystone" or "capstone" that holds the entire arch of the building together. Since the author emphasizes the exaltation of Christ and compares him to the "head" of the entire body of the church (4:15-16) and explicitly says that "whole building is joined together in him," the latter meaning is probable (2:20). Furthermore, "God's household" grows into a "temple that is dedicated to the Lord," "a place where God lives" (2:21-22). The notion of the community as a living temple is also found in Paul, who refers to the individual believer as a "temple of the Holy Spirit" (see 1 Cor 3:16; 6:19-20), which is beautifully elaborated regarding the whole community in 1 Peter 2:4-10.

From the powerful images of this passage, with their emphasis on reconciliation and on the sacredness of the community as a "temple," as the "household" and "a place where God lives," the author of Ephesians will urge his community to "to live as people worthy of the call you received from

God" (4:1), a life expressed especially in mutual love and unity—a motif that runs throughout the remaining portions of the letter. The love of Christ for us expressed in his death on the cross is a revelation of the love of God for us, and, in turn, this lavish and reconciling love is to set the pattern for the life of the church and its witness to the world.

II. The Letter to the Hebrews: Enduring the Cross

The saving effect of Christ's death is the central focus of the Letter to the Hebrews but the word "cross" is found only once in this unique New Testament book. Yet from the content of Hebrews 12:1-3, where Jesus' death on the cross is cited, one can gain an insight into the entire letter.

Although at times attributed to Paul the apostle, the unique style and theology of this work have little in common with the Pauline literature. It is impossible to identify the author with any confidence. For a majority of interpreters, the intended audience of Hebrews is a community with a majority of Jewish Christians, perhaps in the region of Rome (see the reference "the group from Italy greets you" in 13:24), but since there is no clear indication in the letter about these things, these solutions remain hypothetical.[25]

There is more clarity about the fundamental purpose of Hebrews. The author clearly wants to encourage his fellow Christians to deepen their faith and to persevere in spite of the threats they face.[26] The community addressed had apparently undergone some persecution in the past (10:32), a persecution in the form of public abuse and harassment, including even imprisonment and seizure of their possessions (10:33-34). It is possible that the author believes that more of this lies ahead for the community (see, e.g., the reference to those who are now in prison and have been tortured in 13:3). Another concern, perhaps not unrelated, is that some in the community seem to have lost their earlier fervor and some are discouraged and others seem to be distancing themselves from the community (10:25). Others have lost their confidence (10:35) and are facing the uncertain future with "drooping hands" and "weak knees" (12:12).

The ultimate purpose of Hebrews is to urge the Christians to lift up their heads beyond their present concerns and their religious torpor and to view the full vision of their destiny. To do this, the author reminds the community

---

25. See the thorough discussion in Attridge, *Hebrews*, 1–13.

26. Some speculate, in fact, that the literary genre of Hebrews derives from a homily or exhortatory sermon: see Mitchell, *Hebrews*, 13–17, who concludes that Hebrews did originate as a homily with a strong degree of "exhortation," thus fitting the author's own description of his work as a "message of encouragement" (13:22).

107

of the death and exaltation of Jesus Christ, who is both the author of their salvation and the supreme witness of perseverance. At the outset, the letter proclaims that Jesus is God's Son, "the light of God's glory and the imprint of God's being" (1:3). And God, who had spoken to the "ancestors" through the prophets, now definitively speaks to the world through the Son (1:1-2). Thus Hebrews, as had been the case with all of the texts we have examined, portrays God as the one who initiates human salvation as an act of revelation and love.

The distinctiveness of Hebrews is that it chooses to describe the redemptive work of Jesus through an elaborate set of metaphors drawn from the sacrificial liturgy of the Jerusalem temple, in particular the ritual of Yom Kippur, the Day of Atonement. Each of the essential elements of this temple liturgy is metaphorically transformed to illustrate the scope and efficacy of Jesus' death and resurrection. Thus the "temple" involved is not the one built of stone in Jerusalem (which may no longer have been standing at the time the letter was being written) but the heavenly sanctuary of which the Jerusalem temple was only a foreshadowing (Heb 9:11, 24). Jesus himself is both the priest (9:11) and the sacrificial victim (9:14) of this cosmic liturgy. He is priest not in the line of Aaron as were the former temple priests, but in the line of Melchizedek, thus unique, without predecessor or descendent (7:1-28). Yet, as with the priests of old, Jesus is chosen from among the people and has sympathy with their sufferings (5:1-10).[27] But Jesus is also the sacrificial victim, offering not the blood of animals but his own precious blood as a purification from sin (9:11-14). And unlike the priests of old who had to repeat their supplication year after year, Jesus, the high priest, enters the heavenly sanctuary once and for all—his death and resurrection bringing full redemption (10:1-18).

The outcome of this sacrifice of Jesus the high priest is the establishment of a new and better covenant (Heb 8:6–9:22). Just as the first covenant with Moses was sealed with a sacrifice of the blood "of calves and goats" (9:19) so the blood of Jesus shed on the cross initiates the new covenant. The old covenant was not able to remove transgressions, but the covenant forged by the sacrifice of Christ's death is able to "wash our consciences clean from dead works in order to serve the living God" (9:14).

This elaboration of the meaning of Jesus' redemptive work as a journey from death to ultimate life with God forms the foundation for the letter's encouragement of the community, whose hope and courage are frail. This

---

27. In this regard, Hebrews seems to invoke the Gethsemane tradition of Jesus' anguished prayer on the eve of his death where he "offered prayers and requests with loud cries and tears as his sacrifices to the one who was able to save him from death. He was heard because of his godly devotion. Although he was a Son, he learned obedience from what he suffered. After he had been made perfect, he became the source of eternal salvation for everyone who obeys him" (5:7-9).

is precisely the point where the author explicitly refers to the cross of Jesus in Hebrews 12:2. Although snatches of encouragement and exhortation are found throughout the early chapters of the letter (see, e.g., 10:19-25), beginning with Hebrews 12 this becomes an intense focus. In a magnificent rhetorical flourish in the preceding chapter, the author names a catalogue of Old Testament characters whose lives were charged with faith—moving from Abel through Moses and the prophets. From that great "cloud of witnesses" the author turns now at the beginning of Hebrews 12 to the supreme witness, Jesus himself:

> So then let's also run the race that is laid out in front of us, since we have such a great cloud of witnesses surrounding us. Let's throw off any extra baggage, get rid of the sin that trips us up, and fix our eyes on Jesus, faith's pioneer and perfecter. He endured the cross, ignoring the shame, for the sake of the joy that was laid out in front of him, and sat down at the right side of God's throne. (12:1-2)

The author uses athletic imagery throughout this section of the letter—a literary device found frequently in exhortations within Greco-Roman literature.[28] The scene evoked is a great stadium at the end of a marathon; the crowds—"a great cloud of witnesses"—are present to encourage those who run the race. The Greek term *agōn* used here literally means a "contest," but the context identifies it as a race. Like any long-distance runner (ancient and modern) the Christians are urged to lay aside any extra weight or burden—particularly that of sin "that trips us up"—to enable them to better persevere in "the race that is laid out in front of us" (12:1).

The model in this race, which is life's journey, is Jesus himself. The Christians are urged to keep their eyes fixed on the figure of Jesus—a beautiful image of Christian discipleship. He is the "pioneer"—the Greek word *archēgos* can mean the "founder," the "inspirer," that is, the one who initiates or leads (see also 2:10)—and who is the "perfecter" or "completer" of our faith. The Greek word for the latter is *teleiōtēs*, from the root word for "end" or "completion" (*telos*). Here again the fundamental metaphors of Hebrews are at work. Jesus as the Son who is the saving Word of God sent to us and who is the eternal high priest who enters the sanctuary to offer the definitive sacrifice of salvation is indeed the "pioneer" of our faith. And as the one who perseveres through death to life and leads us into the heavenly sanctuary to the right hand of God he is indeed the "completer" or "perfecter" of our faith. Jesus is the *prodromos*, the one who runs through and enters into the sanctuary first

28. See Attridge, *Hebrews*, 354–56.

on our behalf (Heb 6:20). And, in the athletic terms the author now uses at the beginning of Hebrews 12, Jesus, through his death and resurrection, is the one who begins the great race or journey of life for us and runs ahead of us to complete the race and show the way to life eternal.

The essential experience in Jesus' role as "pioneer" and "perfecter" is his death on the cross and its outcome in resurrection. The author captures in a unique way the experience of Jesus Crucified: "For the sake of the joy that was set before him," Jesus "endured the cross" (Heb 12:2). The Greek preposition *anti*, translated here as "for the sake of," can also mean "in place of." In the latter sense, the meaning might be that Jesus, as portrayed in the hymn of Philippians 2, lays aside the joy that was his at the right hand of the Father and submits to death on the cross. More likely, though, in a context that speaks of reaching the goal or the end of the race, is the meaning "for the sake of." Jesus endures the cross because he can anticipate the "joy" of being united through resurrection with his Father in the heavenly sanctuary, just as the Christians themselves are being urged by the author to persevere in view of the glorious goal set before them. Therefore, Jesus "disregards" or "ignores" (the sense of the Greek verb *kataphronēsas*) the shame that is inherent in the cross. Here the author cites a fact that all of his audience would understand—crucifixion was a hideous form of death meant to shame its victim.[29]

In accord with the elaborate metaphor of the heavenly temple ritual that expresses the Christology of Hebrews, the outcome of Jesus' death on the cross is that he "sat down at the right side of God's throne" (12:2).[30] Here is the "joy" that belongs to the resurrected Christ, and this is the destiny of those who believe in him. The author encourages his community to consider the hope of attaining this same "joy" and thereby to live courageously and faithfully in spite of the threats they face. Like Jesus who suffered "outside the city gate"—again showing awareness on the part of the author of the historical circumstances of crucifixion—the Christians should now "go to him outside the camp, bearing his shame" (13:12-13).

III. The First Letter of Peter: The Example of Christ's Sufferings

The First Letter of Peter is one of the New Testament's most beautiful and eloquent books. Written most probably from Rome in the last quarter of

29. See previously, p. 8.

30. The author once again cites Ps 110:1 as he had at the very beginning of Hebrews (see 1:3).

the first century, it is addressed to a series of Christian communities in northern and central Asia Minor, north of the Taurus Mountains.[31] The author is identified as "Peter, an apostle of Jesus Christ" (1:1), and "a fellow elder and a witness of Christ's sufferings" (1 Pet 5:1). While the authorship of the Apostle Peter cannot be ruled out, it is more likely that this letter is written in the apostle's name by a later disciple or a member of a "Petrine group," a group of church elders who felt some pastoral responsibility to the churches addressed.[32]

The Context and Purpose of the Letter

The author clearly identifies the purpose of his letter as one of encouragement (1 Pet 5:12). It is, then, less of a theological treatise than a pastoral response to the situation of the churches addressed. Some indication of that situation is found in the author's address to the recipients as "God's chosen strangers in the world" (literally, "of the diaspora" [1:1]) and as "aliens and exiles" (2:11 AT). Traditional interpretation of 1 Peter understood these terms in a purely spiritual sense, namely that the Christians were "in exile" from our heavenly home. While this meaning may not be all together absent, it is probable that the author is also thinking of the actual social circumstances of these communities.[33] It is clear that they are suffering some alienation and harassment from the surrounding non-Christian majority. They have been branded as evildoers (2:12) and "maligned" and abused because of their "good lifestyle" (3:16). This may be due to resentment that these Christians no longer join with their non-Christian contemporaries "with the same flood of unrestrained wickedness" (4:4). The Christians are to refrain from what their pagan counterparts like to do: "Living in their unrestrained immorality and lust, their drunkenness and excessive feasting and wild parties, and their forbidden worship of idols" (4:3).

While this sort of abuse and isolation carries its own form of suffering, the author seems to believe that this accumulated resentment will eventually erupt into full-blown persecution. He warns them not to be "surprised about the fiery trials that have come among you to test you" (1 Pet 4:12). Lurking

---

31. On the background and context of 1 Peter, see Achtemeier, *1 Peter*, 23–36; J. Elliott, *I Peter*, 84–103; Senior and Harrington, *1 Peter, Jude and 2 Peter*, 4–16. Most interpreters understand the reference, "The fellow-elect church in Babylon greets you" (5:13) as a reference to Rome.

32. See the extended discussion in J. Elliott, *I Peter*, 127–30.

33. Elliott maintains that in addition to the social isolation these Christians experience because of their Christian commitment, they may also have been actual "aliens" who migrated to these regions for work and thus also suffer some ostracism because of this. See J. Elliott, *A Home for the Homeless.*

behind this suffering inflicted on the Christians is the evil power of the demon who is "on the prowl like a roaring lion, seeking someone to devour" (5:8).[34] The Christians of these communities are not alone in their suffering, for their brethren in the whole world are experiencing the same thing (5:9). The elders of the community are to care for the members of their flock and encourage them to "stand firm" in the grace that God gives them (5:12).

Appeal to the Suffering Christ

The author's encouragement of these communities is based on two deeply rooted convictions. First of all, the foundation of the community's identity and hope-filled destiny is made possible through the death and resurrection of Christ. The other is that Jesus' sufferings on the cross not only assure forgiveness and salvation for them but also provide a powerful witness and guide in the midst of their sufferings.

The letter begins by acclaiming the great blessing bestowed on the Christians through the resurrection of Jesus Christ from the dead (1 Pet 1:3-5). Through the paschal mystery, the Christians have received "your salvation" (1:9) and "have been born anew into a living hope" (1:3). They have experienced what the prophets of old announced and into which "angels long to examine" (1:12). The author speaks of the efficacy of Christ's death in sacrificial imagery: they were "not liberated by perishable things like silver or gold from the empty lifestyle you inherited from your ancestors. Instead, you were liberated by the precious blood of Christ, like that of a flawless, spotless lamb" (1:18-19). The suffering and death of Christ freed the Christians from sin—a conviction stated in one of the letter's most eloquent and memorable statements about the efficacy of the cross: "He carried in his own body on the cross the sins we committed. He did this so that we might live in righteousness, having nothing to do with sin. By his wounds you were healed. Though you were like straying sheep, you have now returned to the shepherd and guardian of your lives" (2:24-25).

Throughout the letter the author draws effortlessly on imagery from the Old Testament to describe the sacredness and hope-filled destiny of the now-redeemed Christian community. There is no sense of any tension with Judaism or any reference to past divisions; the author, in effect, speaks of the Christian community as the recipient of all the promises given to God's people. Thus they are being built up into a "spiritual temple" (literally, a "spiritual

---

34. On this, see Horrell, Arnold, and Williams, "Visuality, Vivid Description, and the Message of 1 Peter."

house") made of living stones (2:4-5)—words that almost certainly describe the community as a living temple, a tradition cited also in Ephesians.[35] In accord with their identity as a living temple, the Christians are a "chosen race, a royal priesthood, a holy nation, a people who are God's own" (2:9), a powerful set of images drawn from Exodus 19:6 and Isaiah 43:20.

Thus the author begins by describing beautifully the sacred identity and hope-filled destiny of the Christian community, an identity achieved through the death and resurrection of Jesus. From this basis, the author turns to his work of encouragement, the ultimate purpose of the letter.

The Sufferings of Christ and the Sufferings of the Community

To bolster the community's courage and sustain their hope, the author appeals in a variety of ways to the example of Christ's own sufferings. In comparison with other New Testament books, 1 Peter speaks more frequently of the sufferings of Christ and not simply his death on the cross.[36]

First of all, the author evokes a classic biblical reflection on the meaning that can be found in suffering experienced as a purification or "test": "You now rejoice in this hope, even if it's necessary for you to be distressed for a short time by various trials. This is necessary so that your faith may be found genuine. (Your faith is more valuable than gold, which will be destroyed even though it is itself tested by fire.) Your genuine faith will result in praise, glory, and honor for you when Jesus Christ is revealed" (1 Pet 1:6-7). This strongly echoes the same image of suffering as a purifying trial found in Wisdom 3:4-7. In 1 Peter 4:12-13, the author alludes to the coming "fiery trials" also as a "test," which when successfully endured will lead them to "rejoice as you share Christ's suffering. You share his suffering now so that you may also have overwhelming joy when his glory is revealed."

Even more emphatically the author describes the sufferings of Christ as providing an example of witness that can also give meaning to the sufferings of the Christians. This, in fact, was one of the purposes of Christ's own sufferings: "You were called to this kind of endurance, because Christ suffered on your behalf. He left you an example so that you might follow in his footsteps" (1 Pet 2:21). This call to witness is part of the remarkable overall mission orientation of 1 Peter. Even though the communities addressed seem to be

---

35. Eph 2:19-22. Elliott, however, questions where the term "a spiritual house" (*oikos pneumatikos*) refers to the temple and prefers the literal meaning of a "household" or a human community; see J. Elliott, *I Peter*, 412–18.

36. See 1 Pet 1:11; 2:23; 4:13; 5:1.

under siege from the surrounding hostile culture and suffer abuse and slander, the author does not call for the Christians to retreat into a defensive crouch but to let their forbearance and the inherent goodness of the community and its corporate life be a quiet refutation of the slander they suffer and a witness that could possibly win over those who now attack them.

As examples for the entire community the author singles out two of the most vulnerable groups in the community: slaves (who probably had non-Christian masters) and the wives of non-Christian husbands. In a patriarchal society where the head of the household determined the religious persuasion and the social relationships of its members, these two groups of people were in particularly difficult circumstances if their participation in the Christian community was not shared by the "*pater familias*."[37] The author encourages the slaves to accept the authority of their masters, even abusive ones, "with all respect" (1 Pet 2:18). In doing so they become like the suffering Christ who also endured unjust punishment and did not retaliate: "When he was insulted, he did not reply with insults. When he suffered, he did not threaten revenge" (2:23). The author implies that the suffering of the Christian slaves could be somehow redemptive for others just as Christ's sufferings were— "Christ himself suffered on account of sins, once for all, the righteous one on behalf of the unrighteous. He did this in order to bring you into the presence of God" (3:18).

Likewise, the wives of non-Christian husbands (i.e., of those who "refuse to believe the word," 1 Pet 3:1) should accept the authority of their husbands and, through "the reverent and holy manner of your lives," their husbands may be "won over" (3:2). Their beauty is not to be found in "stylish hair" or by "wearing gold jewelry or fine clothes" but is found "on the inside, in your hearts, with the enduring quality of a gentle, peaceful spirit. This type of beauty is very precious in God's eyes" (3:3-4).

It is clear that the author lifts up these most vulnerable members as examples for the rest of the community. "Husbands" should act in the same way showing consideration for their wives and paying honor to "the weaker partner" (1 Pet 3:7), and, likewise, "all of you" are to live with love for one another, being "compassionate and modest" (3:8), and as was asked of the slaves and women, "don't pay back evil for evil or insult for insult. Instead, give blessing in return" (3:8-9).

The author walks a fine line here. On the one hand he counsels confor-

---

37. See the comment of Achtemeier: "In this instance, as in the case of Christian slaves, Christian wives here point beyond themselves to the general situation of Christians who find themselves at odds with a society within which they must remain true to their Christian confession, whatever suffering that may bring in its wake" (*1 Peter*, 209).

mity with the surrounding structures of society: slaves are to be submissive to their masters, wives deferential to their husbands, and the entire community absorbing abuse rather than retaliating. Those in civil authority are to be respected, whether the "emperor" or the "governors" (1 Pet 2:13-14). But the author also sets limits to the power of civil authorities. The Christians are exhorted to "honor everyone. Love the family of believers [literally, *adelphotēs*, i.e., the "brotherhood"].... Honor the emperor," but, above all, one is to fear God (2:17).[38] And the ultimate purpose of all this Christian behavior is missionary. The refusal to return abuse for abuse, the example of a community that lives in harmony and mutual love, the proper respect shown to those in authority, and the vibrant life of the community and its hopeful spirit are meant to win over those who now abuse the community in order that the abusers "may be ashamed" (3:15-6) and even glorify God when he comes to judge (2:12). So the Christians are urged, "Whenever anyone asks you to speak of your hope, be ready to defend it. Yet do this with respectful humility, maintaining a good conscience" (3:15-16).

IV. The Book of Revelation: The Victory of the Lamb That Was Slain

The Apocalypse, or book of Revelation, closes the New Testament canon and is unique among all the New Testament books. Its literary genre is a combination of letters to the seven churches, which open the book (2:1–3:22); words of prophecy (1:3); and apocalyptic visions, which run throughout the book.[39] The author, John, describes himself as "your brother who shares with you in the hardship, kingdom, and endurance that we have in Jesus." He is apparently in exile on the island of Patmos "because of the word of God and my witness about Jesus" (1:9). John further testifies that he was instructed to write to the seven churches and to reveal what he saw in a vision (1:1-2, 10-11).

The work has a complex structure but its overall format and purpose are clear. Elizabeth Schussler Fiorenza aptly compared it to the fundamental structure and purpose of Dr. Martin Luther King's famous "Letter from a Birmingham Jail." Dr. King, also imprisoned for his faith and witness, writes to his fellow Christians a letter that first of all identifies the evil they face—systemic racism—then sketches a vision of a new world of justice and freedom,

---

38. See Senior and Harrington, *1 Peter, Jude and 2 Peter*, 72–73.

39. For discussion of the literary genre of Revelation, see Robert H. Mounce, *The Book of Revelation*, 1–8.

and concludes by exhorting his fellow Christians to persevere in courage and faith.[40] Similarly, the author of Revelation writes letters of encouragement and challenge to the seven communities of western Asia Minor, naming the demonic power of the Roman Empire as the evil the church faces, drawing a vision of a world redeemed by the blood of the Lamb, and exhorting his fellow Christians to stand fast and not compromise with evil.

Although the book of Revelation has a unique literary form, its fundamental theology of the death and resurrection of Jesus as the source of salvation coincides with the rest of the New Testament, including the Passion Narratives of the gospel literature and the theology of the Pauline and subsequent New Testament writings.[41]

The Context

Interpreters have long debated the original context of Revelation and its significance in discerning the fundamental purpose of the book.[42] It is clear that the intended target of Revelation is the oppressive rule of the Roman Empire. Described alternately as the "beast" (13:1 and numerous other instances) or the "prostitute" (19:2) or "Babylon" (14:8; 16:19; 17:5; 18:2, 10, 21), Rome is indicted for both its economic exploitation (see particularly Rev 18) and for the pretension of its rulers to divine status (13:4, 12; 14:9-11; 17:1). In vivid detail the author describes the impact of Roman taxation and economic oppression delivered by collusion on the part of "the merchants of the earth" (see 18:11). The author clearly considers the power behind Rome's imperial might to be demonic. This is in contrast to such New Testament works as Paul's own letters, the viewpoint of the Pastorals, and the First Letter of Peter—all of which counsel respect for civil authority, despite acknowledging its limits and its potential abuses. But for John, the author of Revelation, no compromise is possible with Roman rule because of its inherently evil and destructive power. Whether or not the Christians in western Asia Minor were being actively persecuted by Rome is debated. Most Christians who went about their lives quietly probably did not experience direct or sustained harassment from Roman authorities. However, the Christians of this region certainly felt the effects of Roman taxation and economic exploitation, and they would have seen signs of the imperial cult proclaiming the divine status of the emperor on many public

---

40. See Schüssler Fiorenza, *Revelation*, 11–12.

41. See Hays, "Faithful Witness, Alpha and Omega," in Hays and Alkier, *Revelation and the Politics of Apocalyptic Interpretation*, 69–83.

42. See the discussion of Revelation's context and purpose in Thompson, *Revelation*, 19–43.

116

buildings and monumental statuary. The author's concern is that the Christian communities he addresses will become complacent in the face of Roman rule and be seduced by it. He urges the Christians not to compromise, for example, by eating meat that had been offered to idols and now was in the marketplace or served at banquets or by participating in any way in the values and rituals of the empire. Their passive resistance to the claims of the empire was meant to be an active testimony to the radically different values and view of life proclaimed by the gospel of Jesus Christ.

While the concern of Revelation is directed to its immediate context and should not be thought of as a detailed prediction of subsequent events of world history, this does not mean that this New Testament book has no contemporary significance. The author's prophetic challenge to injustice, to abusive power, to economic oppression, and to the collusion among exploitive political and economic forces—along with a vision of a world of justice and peace illumined by God's own Spirit—transcends the limits of time and space and can speak to our world of today.

The Lamb That Was Slain

Revelation's prophetic critique of Roman power and its vision of a redeemed world both draw on the author's convictions about the death and resurrection of Christ. The author portrays the saving power of Jesus' death and resurrection in unique imagery. In a pivotal moment in Revelation 5, John at first sees "the Lion of the tribe of Judah, the Root of David" as the one sent by God to conquer evil and deliver God's people (5:1-5), but that image of the lion is transformed into that of the "Lamb standing as if it had been slain" (5:6). The "Lamb" is the Crucified and Risen Christ whose sacrifice "purchased" saints for God "from every tribe, language, people, and nation" (5:9). The multitudes of those saved acclaim, "Worthy is the slaughtered Lamb to receive power, wealth, wisdom, and might, and honor, glory, and blessing" (5:12).

Revelation pits the image of the Lamb who gives his life that others might live over against the image of the "beast" that devours the poor and threatens those who do not worship it (see 13:1-9). That primal beast, which is the Roman Empire, spawns another "beast" that apparently represents all those who advance the power of the first beast by extending its imperial cult and thereby deceiving the inhabitants of the earth (see 13:11-18). Thus the violent "beast" of Rome is defeated not by a counter military force or by imitation of its violence but by the self-transcending and sacrificial love of the Lamb that is Christ.

117

The Christians redeemed by the blood of Christ are described as the multitudes who have "washed their robes and made them white in the Lamb's blood" (Rev 7:14). These are the followers of Jesus who have resisted compromise with evil and have persevered (see also 14:1-5). The author calls "for the endurance of the saints, who keep God's commandments and keep faith with Jesus" (14:12).

The defeat of the beast and the triumph of the Lamb lead to a "new heaven and a new earth" (Rev 21:1). The final segment of Revelation describes in breathtaking terms the beauty of the heavenly Jerusalem, the city of God, that now comes down to earth and becomes the dwelling place of those who have been redeemed by the blood of the Lamb and have persevered in the faith (see Rev 21–22). The temple of this city is "the Lord God the Almighty and the Lamb" (21:22) and for the illumination of this city, "God's glory is its light, and its lamp is the Lamb" (21:23); the water that flows through the city comes "from the throne of God and of the Lamb" and produces the "tree of life" (22:1-2). In this vivid way, the author of Revelation describes not the heavenly realm as such but the complete purification and renewal of the earth itself—a profound transformation not unlike Paul's vision of a newly created world described in Romans 8:18-25, but one utilizing the dramatic apocalyptic imagery unique to Revelation.

Conclusion

The deuteropauline and other New Testament texts we have considered all testify to the belief that the death and resurrection of Christ save humanity from sin and death. Each takes a somewhat different slant on the meaning of the cross for Christian life and each amplifies different dimensions of the meaning of the cross found in the Gospels and in the Pauline literature. For Ephesians and Colossians, the focus is on the cross as an instrument of reconciliation: in the case of Ephesians, the reconciliation between Gentile and Jew that creates one new humanity; for Colossians, a reconciliation of the powers of the universe that takes away fear. Hebrews, 1 Peter, and the book of Revelation draw on the example of the Crucified Christ and the meaning of the cross to encourage Christians under threat but each does so in a distinctive way and in response to the particular circumstances of the communities addressed.

Chapter Six

The Cross and Discipleship

I n virtually all of the New Testament texts we have considered, the cross has profound meaning for Christian life. In some passages, however, a direct line is drawn between the cross and some dimensions of Christian discipleship. It is to these we now turn.

I. Take Up Your Cross and Come Follow Me

The gospel narratives begin the public ministry of Jesus with the call of the first disciples. In the Synoptic Gospels Jesus intrudes into the life of Galilean fishermen and toll collectors and summons them to a new life—"Come, follow me... and I'll show you how to fish for people" (Mark 1:17), implying that the disciples are to follow in the pattern of Jesus' own life and to share in his mission.[1] In John's account, the first disciples are lured to Jesus when he is pointed out by John the Baptist; fascinated by his presence they in turn invite others to "come and see" (1:46).

The implications of what following Jesus and sharing in his mission will entail are spelled out in the challenging discipleship saying of Mark 8:34.[2]

---

1. See Mark 1:16-20; Matt 4:18-22. Luke places their call in a somewhat different setting, incorporating the remarkable catch of fish from Simon's boat; see 5:1-11.

2. See the parallels in Matt 16:24 and Luke 9:23. The saying about "taking up the cross" is repeated in Matt 10:38 and Luke 14:27.

119

When Peter balks at Jesus' first prediction of his passion, Jesus turns to all the disciples and declares, "All who want to come after me must say no to themselves, take up their cross, and follow me."[3] Here the cross and discipleship are bound together. Because crucifixion was well known to first-century Jews as a form of Roman punishment for sedition, it is not impossible that Jesus himself could have spoken of the cross to his disciples in this shocking manner, and it need not be a post-Easter insertion. Jesus' declaration that he had come to proclaim the kingdom of God was a threatening message to imperial authority, and Jesus must have been aware that he faced dangerous opposition. It would not be strange or anachronistic for Jesus to have warned his disciples about the threat of the cross.[4]

However, it is also clear that "taking up the cross" is being presented in the Gospels themselves as a metaphor for discipleship. Luke 9:23, for example, adds the word "daily" to this key saying. To be a follower of Jesus, then and now, means turning away from self-absorption ("say no to themselves") and following Jesus in the manner of his self-transcending love for others, ultimately expressed in the manner of his death. The saying that immediately follows these words of Jesus continues in the same vein: "All who want to save their lives will lose them. But all who lose their lives because of me and because of the good news will save them" (Mark 8:35; see Matt 16:25; Luke 9:24; see also John 12:25).

In another key saying of Jesus in Mark's Gospel, the disciples are urged not to imitate the self-aggrandizement of those who rule among the Gentiles but rather to be the servant of all in the manner of the Son of Man who came not "to be served but rather to serve and to give his life to liberate many people" (10:45).[5] Thus discipleship means not just imitating Jesus in his virtuous life and mission but being willing to give one's life for the other as Jesus did through his death on the cross.

Understanding the death of Jesus on the cross as the supreme expression of his self-transcending love for others is found as well in other key New Testament texts we have considered. Paul, for example, cites an early Christian hymn about Christ putting aside his divine status and, for the sake of his mis-

3. For the sake of inclusive language, the Common English Bible has put this saying in the plural form; the original is singular: "Whoever wants to follow after me, should deny himself and take up his cross and follow me" (AT).

4. On this see the persuasive accumulation of evidence from the Gospels and other New Testament texts brought forward by Allison, *Constructing Jesus: Memory, Imagination, and History*, 427–33. Allison affirms that the historical Jesus not only was aware of his likely death but also accepted it as part of God's mysterious plan. See also the remarks of Moloney, who interacts with Allison's view that Jesus anticipated his death and accepted it as ultimately life giving, "Constructing Jesus and the Son of Man." Also see Meier, *A Marginal Jew*, vol. 3, *Companions and Competitors*, 64–65, who also argues for Jesus as the original source of the saying.

5. See discussion of this text previously, pp. 33–34.

sion from God, becoming human, even to the point of death on the cross.[6] Paul's reason for citing this hymn is to urge the Christians at Philippi to turn away from factionalism and to be committed to each other in love: "Don't do anything for selfish purposes but with humility think of others as better than yourselves. Instead of each person watching out for their own good, watch out for what is better for others" (Phil 2:3-4). For Paul this was equivalent to "adopt[ing] the attitude that was in Christ Jesus"—the "attitude" manifested in his death on the cross (Phil 2:5).

The Johannine tradition also moves in this same direction. Jesus' command to his disciples at the last discourse is "to love each other just as I have loved you" (John 15:12, 17). The manner of that love is spelled out: "No one has greater love than to give up one's life for one's friends. You are my friends if you do what I command you" (15:13-14). John's Gospel presents the death of Jesus on the cross as an act of friendship love, a love stated at the outset of the final discourse: "Having loved his own who were in the world, he loved them fully" (13:1, literally, "to the end").[7]

Describing Christian discipleship as "taking up the cross" in the manner of Jesus' self-transcending love and such phrases as "denying oneself" or "becoming a servant" or "slave" must not be understood in a servile and demeaning manner. Feminist theologians and others have raised this legitimate concern because, at times, such gospel sayings have been manipulated to hold others in submission or to encourage passivity.[8] To love another does not mean one denigrates or submerges one's own dignity as a human being, nor does it encourage a passive or subservient stance. The startling rhetoric used in Jesus' sayings about discipleship challenges a toxic self-absorption, an inability to look beyond oneself and to seek the good of the other.

To love as Jesus loved has been exemplified in the gracious, enduring, and mature love of Christians over the ages: parents, spouses, teachers, friends, those who are willing on a daily basis or in moments of intense and heroic generosity to give their lives for the other. This is what is meant by "taking up one's cross and following Jesus."

II. Various Modalities of Taking Up the Cross

Discipleship lived in the light of the cross takes various forms or expressions across the New Testament, depending on the purpose and context of the particular passage.

---

6. See earlier, p. 13.

7. On the Johannine interpretation of the death of Jesus, see previously, pp. 62–76.

8. See earlier, pp. xvi–xvii.

The Cross and Perseverance in the Face of Suffering and Persecution

Several New Testament texts evoke the cross as encouragement for perseverance and fidelity in the face of suffering and persecution. The portrayal of Jesus himself in the gospel Passion Narratives is one of constancy in the midst of suffering. Despite betrayal and an unjust arrest, despite abandonment by his own followers, despite false accusations, torture, and unjust condemnation, the Jesus of the Gospels remains faithful. At the outset of the passion account, Jesus in Gethsemane prays for deliverance from death, but his fidelity to God's will is even more urgent.[9] Matthew's account, as we saw, emphasizes Jesus' trust even in the midst of anguish, reciting the lament of Psalm 22 as he gives over his life breath (27:50). In Luke, Jesus is portrayed as the faithful martyr who urges his own disciples to persevere, designating them as "the ones who have continued with me in my trials" (22:28). In John's Gospel, Jesus will continue his mission of revealing God's love to the very end (13:1-2), dying with the words, "It is completed" (19:30).

The diverse portrayals of Jesus at the very moment of his death in the Passion Narratives are themselves meant as encouragement to Christians in their own encounter with suffering and death. These differences are, in fact, striking and we have noted some of them in our previous discussion of the gospel passion accounts.[10] In Mark's Gospel, for example, Jesus dies with a wordless scream, literally, "But Jesus let out a loud cry and died" (literally, "expired"; *ho de Iēsous apheis phōnēn megalēn exepneusen*; 15:37). The moment of his death is stark and unadorned; he has given his life in the midst of mockery and abuse. Matthew's account brings a greater sense of order or control to this moment; Jesus dies repeating the words of the lament psalm: "My God, my God, why have you left me?" and then literally, "yields" or "hands over his spirit" (*aphēken to pneuma*; 27:46, 50 AT), implying a final act of obedience and trust in the God to whom his life breath belonged.[11] Luke, whose Passion Narrative portrays Jesus as prophet and martyr who faces suffering heroically, reflects this in his description of Jesus' last moment (23:46). Jesus' last words are from Psalm 31:6. He cries out, "Father, *into your hands I entrust my life*" (literally, "my spirit" [*pneuma*]; Luke 23:46), and with those words of trust, Jesus expires. And finally, John gives the moment of Jesus' death a sense of serene triumph, reflective of his Passion Narrative as a whole. With his final breath, Jesus declares, "It is completed," and then "bowing his head,

---

9. Mark 14:32-42; Matt 26:36-46; Luke 22:39-46. John's Gospel seems to have transposed this tradition in 12:27-33, and it is echoed in Heb 5:7-9.

10. See earlier, pp. 29–77.

11. On this interpretation, see previously, p. 48.

he gave up his life" (literally, "handed over his spirit"; *paredōken to pneuma*; John 19:30).

In these four accounts, death comes to Jesus in various ways: in the midst of stark anguish; with a sense of lament yet trusting in God's fidelity; with exemplary courage and confidence in God; with a sense of completion and serenity. Surely each of these portrayals of Jesus' sufferings and final encounter with death was meant to exemplify how the followers of Jesus can encounter death with integrity. In effect, the gospel accounts assure the Christian that there is not one "model" way to face death but many different ways to enter into the mystery of death with fidelity.

This example of Jesus' own perseverance in the midst of suffering stands behind other New Testament texts that appeal to the cross as encouragement in the face of suffering and death. In the case of the Letter to the Hebrews, the Christian community addressed is apparently weary from enduring harassment and even imprisonment, and some have backed away from involvement in the community. As the author picturesquely describes their situation, they have "drooping hands and weak knees" (12:12). Hebrews lifts up the example of Jesus, the high priest who is the "pioneer" and "perfecter," or completer, of our salvation (2:10; 12:2). Jesus is the one who runs first (*prodromos*) into the sanctuary leading the way for the rest of us (Heb 6:20). To offer his readers the full sense of Christ's redemptive work, the letter elaborates the metaphor of the great heavenly liturgy in which Jesus is both priest and victim, entering the heavenly sanctuary and offering an acceptable sacrifice to God on our behalf.

The ultimate purpose of the letter, however, is to encourage the Christians addressed to persevere in the manner of Jesus' own perseverance on the cross. The faithful saints of the Old Testament form a "cloud of witnesses" who exemplify fidelity to God (Heb 12:1), but the supreme example is that of Jesus himself in his endurance of the cross. The Christians are urged "to fix our eyes on Jesus, faith's pioneer and perfecter. He endured the cross, ignoring the shame, for the sake of the joy that was laid out in front of him, and sat down at the right side of God's throne" (12:2).[12] Here both "shame" and "joy" are evoked in connection with the cross. The "shame" of crucifixion would be well known to the Christians of the first century who lived under Roman imperial rule. The "joy" comes from the outcome of Jesus' death in resurrection and union with his Father—it was that sure passage from death to life that the author lifts up before the community as encouragement for their perseverance under suffering.

12. See earlier, pp. 107–10.

123

As we have seen, the First Letter of Peter also has encouragement as one of its main purposes.[13] Here the context is the isolation and abuse the Christians experience in the midst of a surrounding culture that resents their different behavior and slanders and harasses them (4:3-4). The author addresses them as "immigrants" and "strangers" in their own land (1 Pet 2:11). Particularly vulnerable because of their social standing are slaves and the wives of non-Christian husbands. To them and to the entire community, the author commends the example of Jesus, who also endured unjust sufferings:

> You were called to this kind of endurance, because Christ suffered on your behalf. He left you an example so that you might follow in his footsteps. He committed no sin, nor did he ever speak in ways meant to deceive. When he was insulted, he did not reply with insults. When he suffered, he did not threaten revenge. Instead, he entrusted himself to the one who judges justly. He carried in his own body on the cross the sins we committed. He did this so that we might live in righteousness, having nothing to do with sin. By his wounds you were healed. (1 Pet 2:21-24)

The Cross and the Mission of Christian Witness

In a variety of ways, the cross also signifies the Christian responsibility to give witness to the world. This is clear in Paul's writings. The crucifixion of Jesus represented a challenge to worldly wisdom, testifying to the wisdom of God and God's care for the most vulnerable and the despised of this world. In the opening chapters of his First Letter to the Corinthians, Paul turns to the wisdom of the cross as a means of profound challenge to social norms. Greco-Roman society gave high value to "honor"; the seeking of honor was a major concern just as the experience of shame or humiliation was considered abhorrent and a sign of failure.[14] Crucifixion was feared throughout the Mediterranean world not simply because of its cruel manner of inflicting death but because the entire ritual of crucifixion brought degrading public shame on the victim.[15] By revealing God's love for the world through a Crucified Messiah, divine wisdom directly challenged the assumptions of human wisdom that placed supreme value on personal honor. Paul cites three typical positions of honor that exemplified such worldly wisdom: "Where are the wise? Where are the legal experts? Where are today's debaters?" (1 Cor 1:20).

---

13. See previously, pp. 110–15.

14. See Finney, *Honour and Conflict in the Ancient World*, esp. 17–48.

15. See earlier, pp. 1–9.

The apostle reminds the Corinthians that the very make-up of the community itself reveals God's wisdom:

> Look at your situation when you were called, brothers and sisters! By ordinary human standards not many were wise, not many were powerful, not many were from the upper class. But God chose what the world considers foolish to shame the wise. God chose what the world considers weak to shame the strong. And God chose what the world considers low-class and low-life—what is considered to be nothing—to reduce what is considered to be something to nothing. (1 Cor 1:26-28)

Even Paul's own experience as an apostle—his physical and spiritual limitations, his "weakness"—testifies to God's unique wisdom, as he bears the treasure of his apostolic calling in "clay pots." In so doing, Paul claims, "We always carry Jesus' death around in our bodies so that Jesus' life can also be seen in our bodies" (2 Cor 4:7, 10). And similarly Paul would severely critique the community's celebration of the Lord's Supper, where the rich with their ample provisions were willing to embarrass the poor who had little or nothing (1 Cor 11:11-34). Here again he recalls the passion of Jesus as an antidote to such arrogance and disrespect; on the night he was betrayed Jesus spoke of his body that was to be given "for you" and his blood poured out to establish a new covenant (1 Cor 11:24-25). To celebrate the Lord's Supper in memory of the Crucified Jesus while inflicting harm on others was an abomination.

Thus for Paul, the Crucified Jesus, who embodies God's wisdom, stands as a fundamental critique of the vain pursuit of self-aggrandizement and personal honor. What animated Jesus and what reveals the true nature of God is self-transcending love, not self-seeking pride. For Paul this fundamental ethic of the cross was not simply a way of life confined to the community itself, it offered a fundamental critique of the social world of which they were a part.

We can find a similar logic of the cross, although in different terms, in Jesus' challenge to his disciples in Mark's Gospel, with parallels in both Matthew and Luke. Following his final passion prediction on the way to Jerusalem, when Zebedee's sons attempt to claim places of honor when Jesus would enter his glory (Mark 10:35-37), Jesus instructs his disciples not to imitate the arrogance and self-aggrandizements of the Gentile rulers who "show off their authority over" their subjects (literally, "lord it over" their subjects, a rare word used by Mark here, *katakyrieuousin*) but, rather, to serve others in the manner of how the "Human One didn't come to be served but rather to serve, to give his life to liberate many people" (10:42, 45).[16]

---

16. The CEB translation is cited here but the literal rendering of Mark's Greek text is, "The Son of

As we have noted above, the contrast between oppressive power and the life-giving power of the Crucified Christ is an underlying motif of the Passion Narratives, particularly through the motif of "kingship," which dominates the trial before Pilate.[17] The suffering Christ who is mocked by the soldiers and religious authorities for his supposed pretensions to kingship is, in the eyes of faith, truly the royal Son of God and more than a king. The final confrontation is between Pilate, the representative of the emperor, and Jesus, who embodies God's own wisdom.[18] The trappings of kingship that are imposed on Jesus the prisoner—the purple cloak, the crown of thorns, the fake scepter, and mock acts of homage—are turned back in irony on Jesus' tormentors. He truly is, as the placard over his cross proclaims, "king of the Jews" but a king who is like no other—a king who exercises his power in giving his life for the many.

The confrontation between the cross and the empire, which is more subtly stated in Paul and in the Passion Narratives, breaks into the open in the book of Revelation. The author considers the Roman Empire, with its vicious economic exploitation of the poor, its corrupting power that entangles the "merchants of the earth" (Rev 18:3) in its net, and its rulers' blasphemous claims to divine status as symptomatic of its fundamentally demonic nature.[19] Standing behind the evil ways of the empire and its rulers is the "beast" who is diametrically opposed to the "Lamb." John the Seer, who is named as the author of Revelation (Rev 1:1-2) portrays an image of the Crucified Jesus as the "slaughtered Lamb" (Rev 5:12) that sets up a paradoxical and cosmic struggle between the power of evil expressed through the violence and oppression of the Roman Empire and the power of Jesus Crucified, which is the power of integrity, compassion, and self-transcending love. Therefore, there can be no compromise for the Christians—no involvement in the values and customs of the empire, no accommodation to its way of life. The churches addressed at the beginning of Revelation are to retrieve their original fervor and to be steadfast in their faith as a witness of their allegiance to Christ.

Man came not to be served but to serve, to give his life in ransom for the many"; *kai gar ho huios tou anthrōpou ouk ēlthen diakonēthēnai alla diakonēsai kai dounai tēn psychēn autou lytron anti pollōn* (AT). See Matt 20:25-28; Luke has similar words of Jesus but they are found in the setting of the final Passover meal (Luke 22:24-27). As noted previously, Luke does not have an exact parallel to Mark 10:45 (i.e., "to give his life in ransom for the many") but Luke 22:27b evokes the same emphasis on service ("But I am among you as one who serves."). See earlier, pp. 58, 71–72.

17. See previously, pp. 58, 71–72.

18. This is a particular emphasis of John's Passion Narrative; see earlier, pp. 71–72.

19. This is especially strong in Rev 17–19. See further, Kraybill, *Apocalypse and Allegiance*; see also Wright, "Revelation and Christian Hope: Political Implications of the Revelation to John," in Hays and Alkier, *Revelation and the Politics of Apocalyptic Interpretation*, 1105–24. For a general overview of the relationship of early Christianity and the New Testament writings to the Roman Empire, see Carter, *The Roman Empire and the New Testament*.

While the apocalyptic style of Revelation sets up a cosmic dualism between good and evil, the outcome is not in doubt. The Lamb that was slain triumphs over the beast in all its manifestations and ushers in a "new heaven and a new earth." The world that had been trampled and despoiled by the despotic exploitations of the empire is now renewed and becomes the "New Jerusalem" aglow with beauty and life (Rev 21:1-2). The "great crowd" who washed their robes in the blood of the Lamb (Rev 7:1-17), are those "who hold firmly to the witness of Jesus" (19:10), those "who had been beheaded for their witness to Jesus and God's word, and those who hadn't worshipped the beast or its image, who hadn't received the mark on their forehead or hand" (20:4)—these are the ones who will rule with the triumphant Lamb in the new world redeemed by the blood of Christ.

Both the book of Revelation and the First Letter of Peter call for public witness in the face of the wider culture, but there is a remarkable contrast between the two. Where the book of Revelation names the opposition demonic and calls for uncompromising resistance, the author of 1 Peter takes a gentler tactic.[20] The letter even calls for the Christians out of respect to "submit" to the authority of the emperor and to the Roman governors who rule in his name (2:13-17). In response to the slander and isolation the community experiences because of its Christian commitment and its refusal to lead the corrupt lifestyle of many of its neighbors, the author urges the community members to give witness for their way of life—the reason for their hope (3:15)—but to do so with "respectful humility, maintaining a good conscience" (3:16; literally 1 Peter's Greek text reads, "with humility and fear." The Greek term is *phobos*, literally meaning "fear" but here implying religious "fear" or "reverence"). The intent is that in seeing the goodness of the Christians, those who have been slandering them will be won over. Those disciples in circumstances where they are particularly vulnerable to abuse—slaves and the wives of non-Christian husbands—are to employ the same strategy of nonconfrontation but with the witness of steadfast goodness and virtue (see 1 Pet 2:18–3:6). These and all the members of the community are to refrain from retaliation or returning insult for insult.

The model for this form of Christian witness is precisely the sufferings of Jesus himself. The Christian is called to

> this kind of endurance, because Christ suffered on your behalf. He left you an example so that you might follow in his footsteps. He committed no sin, nor did he ever speak in ways meant to deceive. When he was insulted, he did not reply with insults. When he suffered, he did not threaten revenge.

---

20. See earlier, pp. 110–18.

127

Instead, he entrusted himself to the one who judges justly. He carried in his own body on the cross the sins we committed. He did this so that we might live in righteousness, having nothing to do with sin. By his wounds you were healed. (1 Pet 2:21-24)

The Cross and the Nature of the Christian Community

Finally we turn to a focus on the communal dimension of Christian discipleship. "Taking up one's cross and following after Jesus" is not simply a call for the individual Christian but also shapes the life of the Christian community. What sort of community lives in the shadow of the cross? In what ways does the New Testament link the cross of Christ and the qualities of the Christian community?

A Community Reconciled to God

Paul speaks of reconciliation in his Second Letter to the Corinthians (see particularly 5:18-21). By "reconciliation" the apostle means God's freely given gift of freedom from sin and alienation. "In other words," Paul affirms, "God was reconciling the world to himself through Christ, by not counting people's sins against them" (2 Cor 5:19). Paul is also clear that the instrumentality through which God effected this reconciliation was the death of Jesus on the cross that revealed God's love for the world: "The love of Christ controls us, because we have concluded this: one died for the sake of all; therefore, all died. He died for the sake of all so that those who are alive should live not for themselves but for the one who died for them and was raised" (5:14-15). Because of God's reconciling love, the Christian is a "new creation" (5:17). This fundamental message is at the heart of Paul's own calling as an apostle. God has given him "the ministry of reconciliation"—he was to be an ambassador of Christ (5:18, 20), that is, to announce God's liberating love of the world expressed through the cross of Christ.

In the letters to the Colossians and Ephesians, this Pauline conviction of God's reconciling work is amplified and connected to the life of the community. Colossians affirms that God's triumph over sin and evil through the cross of Christ extends even to the alien powers of the universe. Through his death on the cross, Christ disarmed the powers of the universe that threatened humanity and triumphed over them (Col 2:15); through his death he nullified any indictment imposed on humanity, nailing the document to the cross (2:14). By removing this cosmic threat, the reconciling cross of Christ dissolves fear and brings "peace" (1:20). On this basis, Colossians urges the community to live a life that reflects this new reality; they are to set aside things "such as anger, rage, malice, slander, and obscene language. Don't lie to each other. Take off the old human nature with its practices and put on the new nature, which is renewed in knowledge by conforming to the image of the one who created it. In this image there is neither Greek nor Jew, circumcised nor uncircumcised, barbarian, Scythian, slave nor free, but Christ is all things and in all people" (3:8-11).

Relationships within the community reflect the love and peace that Christ made possible for them:

Therefore, as God's choice, holy and loved, put on compassion, kindness, humility, gentleness, and patience. Be tolerant with each other and, if someone has a complaint against anyone, forgive each other. As the Lord forgave you, so also forgive each other. And over all these things put on love, which is the perfect bond of unity. The peace of Christ must control your hearts—a peace into which you were called in one body. (Col 3:12-15)

The Letter to the Ephesians works within the same framework of reconciliation as Colossians but, as we have seen, focuses on the historic division between Jew and Gentile. Christ's death breaks down that separation:

Christ is our peace. He made both Jews and Gentiles into one group. With his body, he broke down the barrier of hatred that divided us. He canceled the detailed rules of the Law so that he could create one new person out of the two groups, making peace. He reconciled them both as one body to God by the cross, which ended the hostility to God. (Eph 2:14-16)[21]

The community is to be "one body" of which Christ is the head (Eph 4:15-16) and, therefore, is to reflect that hard-won reconciliation in the manner of its communal life. The Christians are asked to "conduct yourselves with all humility, gentleness, and patience. Accept each other with love, and make an effort to preserve the unity of the Spirit with the peace that ties you together. You are one body and one spirit just as God also called you in one hope. There is one Lord, one faith, one baptism, and one God and Father of all, who is over all, through all, and in all" (Eph 4:2-6).

A Community Bound Together in Self-Transcending Love

Across the ensemble of New Testament texts there is a remarkable consistency in exhortations about the qualities that should characterize relationships

21. For an analysis of this passage, see previously, pp. 104–6.

within the community. Time and again, the Pauline Letters, the deuteropauline materials and the other remaining texts of the New Testament speak of the need to refrain from factions and rivalries,[22] to avoid harsh words and recriminations, to speak with graciousness and mutual respect, to surmount differences, to be ready to forgive, to be immersed in peace, to love one another.[23]

Without doubt this vision of the Christian community is rooted in the teachings of Jesus himself and in the heritage of Judaism upon which Jesus drew, with its emphasis on the covenant and its obligations of mutual respect, justice, and compassion. The Gospels testify that Jesus' own teaching placed particular emphasis on forgiveness and care for those in need. The fusion of the command to love God and to love one's neighbor is seen as a characteristic and distinct teaching of the historical Jesus.[24] Likewise, his signature teaching on love of enemies is portrayed by Matthew as the supreme example of Jesus' interpretation of the law (5:43-48). The emphasis on forgiveness is found in all three Synoptic Gospels, including the exhortation in Matthew 18:21-22 to forgive "seventy-seven times." In the Johannine tradition, the commands of Jesus to his disciples are distilled into the one love command: "Love each other as I have loved you."[25]

But beyond this teaching tradition, the supreme example of the quality of love that is to characterize the Christian community is found in the manner of Jesus' death. Jesus' death on the cross is understood by virtually every New Testament tradition as an unimpeachable example of self-transcending love—a love that was expressed throughout the ministry of Jesus and a love that revealed God's own redemptive love for the world. Thus Paul, in urging the Christian community of Philippi to avoid factions and to love each other, appeals to the "attitude that was in Christ Jesus," an attitude eloquently expressed in his putting aside his own interests and humbling himself "by becoming obedient to the point of death, even death on a cross" (Phil 2:5-

22. See 1 Cor 1:10-17; Rom 15:5; Gal 5:13-15; Phil 2:1-4; Col 2:16-19; Eph 2:11-22; Titus 3:10-11.

23. Such exhortations abound in the New Testament: see, e.g., Rom 12:9-21; 15:5-6; 1 Cor 12:31–13:13; 2 Cor 13:11-12; Eph 4:1-16, 31-32; 5:18-20; Phil 4:8-9; Col 3:5-17; 1 Thess 4:9-12; 5:11, 12-22; 2 Tim 2:22-26; Heb 13:1-16; 1 Pet 3:8-9; 4:7-11. Jesus' own words about forgiveness play a prominent role in the Sermon on the Mount: e.g., Matt 5:21-24, 43-48; 6:12, 14; see also the emphasis on forgiveness in the so-called community discourse of Matt 18 (18:21-35).

24. John Meier contends that the double love command taught by Jesus that combined Deut 6:4-5 ("Love the Lord your God with all your heart, all your being, and all your strength") and Lev 19:18 ("You must love your neighbor as yourself") was an innovation within Jewish tradition; see *A Marginal Jew*, vol. 4, *Law and Love*, 499–528.

25. See John 13:34-35; 15:12-17. This Johannine formulation is clearly present in 1 John as well: see, e.g., 3:16, 23; 4:11, 20-21.

11). Therefore, the cross of Christ, because of the quality of love it expressed, becomes the norm for the life and witness of the communities formed in Jesus' name.

The Crucified Body of Christ: The Humanity of the Church

There is another important dimension of Christian community life that finds its source in the cross of Christ. From the outset, Paul draws from the cross a "theology of weakness."[26] The wisdom of God who effects human salvation through a Crucified Messiah confounds human wisdom and embraces those who are the least, the "foolish" and the "weak" of this world (1 Cor 1:26-27). Paul considers both the low social standing of the Corinthian community itself and his own "weakness" as testimony to God's gracious love of the "ungodly" (Rom 4:5).

Thus the church founded in the name of the Crucified Christ is not a community of the elite but a church of the "least," a community of sinners who, without merit, have received the gracious and indiscriminate love of God that has taken away their sins and reconciled them to God ("while we were still sinners..."; Rom 5:8). This sense of humility, and the spirit of compassion and forgiveness that should flow from it, is apparent in several dimensions of the New Testament's portrayal of the Christian community.

The Gospels, for example, portray the disciples of Jesus—representative as they are of the later generations of Jesus' followers—not as an alert and ideal group but as ones who are often baffled by Jesus' teaching, who are either lacking faith (Mark 4:40) or at least "weak in faith" (see Matt 6:30; 16:8), and who misunderstand and sometimes even oppose Jesus' mission. At the same time the Gospels underscore the dignity and privilege of those first called to follow Jesus and who are entrusted with his mission of teaching and healing, they also paint a picture of the spiritual weakness and frailty of the community Jesus forms. Mark's Gospel presents the weakness of the disciples in the starkest terms: their initial lack of understanding of Jesus' parables (4:13) and of his extraordinary miracles such as the multiplication of the loaves and the walking on the water (6:51-52) climaxes in Jesus' frustration at their obtuseness (8:14-21). But as Jesus turns to Jerusalem and begins to speak of his impending passion and death, their initial lack of understanding turns to opposition as Peter attempts to silence Jesus' prediction (8:32-33) and the other disciples argue over who is the greatest and seek positions of power when Jesus should come into his kingdom (9:33-34; 10:35-41).

Faced with the specter of Jesus' death and sensing their own danger, these

---

26. See earlier, pp. 83–88.

same disciples will betray, deny, and flee from Jesus at the time of his greatest need. The closer the cross of Christ looms, the more apparent becomes the weakness of the disciples. For Mark's Gospel, the message of the Risen Christ, transmitted through the heavenly messenger at the empty tomb and carried to the disciples through the women who had stood by Jesus, is one of forgiveness for their failures and renewal of their discipleship. In John 21, in the aftermath of the resurrection, the Risen Jesus heals Peter's denial by drawing from him a poignant threefold affirmation of his love, thereby restoring his vocation "to feed my sheep" (21:15-19).

What is presented in such stark terms by Mark's Gospel is moderated by Matthew and Luke, but the basic portrayal is the same.[27] The chosen disciples of Jesus are not perfect but clearly human and subject to weakness and failure. In John's Gospel, too, the disciples are portrayed as lacking mature faith in Jesus and not yet fully understanding his teaching. And when Jesus speaks of giving his body for the life of the world, many of his followers leave him because of this "harsh" message (6:60-66).[28] For each of the gospels the passion and death of Jesus becomes the ultimate stumbling block. Despite their bravado at the Last Supper, where Peter and the rest swear they will stand by Jesus, they ultimately fail.[29] With the exception of the Beloved Disciple who is present at the cross in John's account, along with the mother of Jesus and the other women witnesses (John 19:25-27), no male disciple who was expressly called by Jesus stands by him at the cross.[30] Only the faithful women who had followed Jesus from Galilee to Jerusalem and attended to his needs remain present (Mark 15:40-41; Matt 27:55-56; Luke 23:49).

Thus the community of disciples portrayed in the Gospels is an imperfect and very human community, prone to weakness and failure, a failure that becomes acute under the shadow of the cross. No doubt it is this human dimension of the followers of Jesus, who, despite their faith in him, remain weak, that is reflected in the New Testament emphasis on forgiveness and compassion found in the teachings of Jesus himself and in the exhortations

27. Matthew, e.g., uses the term "little faith" (*oligopistoi*) where Mark will characterize the disciples as having no faith; see, e.g., Matt 8:26; 14:31; 17:20. As we have noted, Luke does not comment on the flight of the disciples at the moment of Jesus' arrest, and Jesus addresses them as "ones who have continued with me in my trials" (22:28), anticipating their key transitional role from the Gospel to Acts.

28. On this aspect of John's portrayal of the disciples as lacking full faith, see Farelly, *The Disciples in the Fourth Gospel*.

29. Note Peter's confident statement: "But Peter insisted, 'If I must die alongside you, I won't deny you.' And they all said the same thing" (Mark 14:31; Matt 26:35). Luke even has an argument break out at the Supper (22:24), a text found in Mark's Gospel on the road to Jerusalem (9:34)!

30. Note that Luke may imply their presence at a distance; see 23:49, which refers to "everyone who knew him" standing at a distance.

of Paul and the other New Testament writers, as cited above.[31] What is the ultimate purpose of this emphasis? Rather than portray the first generation of disciples as ideal and morally perfect, the New Testament presents a picture of a genuinely human community in need of forgiveness and urged to speak and act with compassion and love. Ultimately such an emphasis is itself an act of compassion, allowing the hearers and readers of the Gospels and the other New Testament literature to find themselves and their community in this picture.[32] Rather than facing a community of ideal Christians, they meet a community of real Christians in need of forgiveness and striving to live the gospel in the midst of their human frailty.

This compassionate (and realistic) view of the church is rooted ultimately in the theology of the cross. In one of his most powerful images for the church, Paul reminds the Christians at Corinth and Rome that they are the "body of Christ." This metaphor also finds an echo in Colossians and Ephesians. Paul understands this image not as a simple metaphor but as a profound metaphysical reality. Through baptism Christians are "in Christ," immersed in his death and resurrection, radically transformed by his grace, and thus truly bound to each other: "If one part suffers, all the parts suffer with it; if one part gets the glory, all the parts celebrate with it" (1 Cor 12:26).

Yet it is important to ask what kind of a body Paul imagines when he speaks of the church as the "body of Christ." Is it a perfectly portioned and toned body, a body expressing the ideals of Greco-Roman art? Or is it, rather, the crucified and wounded body of Christ that Paul has in mind? There is reason to believe that in fact Paul is contemplating the Crucified Christ when he thinks of the church. Some hint of that is found in 1 Cor 12:22-27 when Paul notes that in the body of Christ,

> the parts of the body that people think are the weakest are the most necessary. The parts of the body that we think are less honorable are the ones we honor the most. The private parts of our body that aren't presentable are the ones that are given the most dignity.... But God has put the body together, giving greater honor to the part with less honor so that there won't be division in the body and so the parts might have mutual concern for each other.

Paul arrives at this passage after having first confronted the problem

---

31. See earlier, p. 87.

32. See Whitaker, "Rebuke or Recall?," who links the emphasis on failure and forgiveness in Mark's portrayal of Peter and the other disciples with the early Christian controversy over the possibility of "second repentance."

with the Corinthian community's celebration of the Eucharist where the rich members were embarrassing the poorest members. To counter this, as we noted above, Paul reminds his community of Jesus' giving of his life symbolized in his breaking of the bread and sharing the cup (see 1 Cor 11:17-34).[33] From this point in his letter he moves to speak of the harmony of gifts that should characterize the community (12:1-11) and then presents the image of the church as the body of Christ. This section of the letter leads to 1 Corinthians 13, the extraordinary "hymn to charity" where Paul spells out the quality of the self-transcending and gracious love that should characterize relationships within the church of Christ. Driving Paul's entire portrayal of the Christian community is his theology of the cross in which the quality of God's love has been revealed through the love that animated the Crucified Christ, a love that is gracious, self-transcending, and reaches out to those who are the least.

What Paul does discursively in his letter may also be the point of the haunting image of the Risen Christ presented in the concluding appearance scenes of Luke and John's Gospels. The Risen Christ still bears his wounds in his hands and feet and side (see Luke 23:39-40; John 20:20, 25-27). The Gospels want to emphasize that the Risen Christ is indeed the Crucified Christ. It is the Crucified Christ, who gave his life for sinners and identified with the "least," who remains with the church and whose spirit of forgiveness, compassion, and gracious love characterizes the community that bears the name *the body of Christ*.

---

33. See earlier, p. 94.

Conclusion

Do This in Memory of Me

The guiding question of this study has been: Why the cross? Our exploration of the New Testament has yielded multiple answers to this question.

Why the cross? Because, in fact, Jesus of Nazareth was crucified in Jerusalem by Roman authorities in the first third of the first century. He suffered what the ancient world considered a particularly heinous form of capital punishment—one meant to be a profound humiliation of its victim and a deterrent to crimes that challenged or disrupted public order and civil authority.

Why the cross? Because Jesus' death by crucifixion was the unimpeachable proof of his humanity. Through his suffering and death on the cross Jesus of Nazareth demonstrates solidarity with all human suffering, especially with innocent suffering, and offers it the possibility of new meaning.

Why the cross? Because Jesus was innocent and just, his death on the cross was an act of supreme injustice, an act of violence and oppression whose roots are radically evil. Because his mission of justice led to his death, the cross also stands, therefore, as a sign of condemnation of all injustice and oppression, of all infliction of violence and suffering on the innocent.

Why the cross? Because the reality of Jesus' death on the cross makes room for the paradox of suffering within human experience. Suffering can be redemptive but human suffering is not to be embraced or condoned as valuable and purifying without the Christian community first standing in opposition to human suffering and seeking to alleviate it. Jesus is, first of all, a healer, determined to overcome human suffering and to liberate humans from the power of sin and death. In the face of death, Jesus is portrayed as lamenting and praying for deliverance.

Why the cross? Because Jesus' death on the cross is recognized as the culminating expression of a life animated by self-transcending love, a love that reveals God's gracious love for humanity and the world God created. That death liberates humans from the burden of sin and death. Through participation in the paschal mystery the Christian shares in Jesus' own victory over death and is reconciled with God.

Why the cross? Because through the crucifixion of Jesus, Christ and Son of God, we come to realize that the wisdom of God is different from human wisdom and that God's ways are not our ways. Through the cross we recognize the God who cares for those who are poor and vulnerable, the God of the "ungodly," the God who embraces all peoples.

Why the cross? Because in "taking up the cross and following Jesus" Christians through grace are able to shape their lives in the pattern of Jesus' own life-giving mission: animated by self-transcending love, serving rather than being served, giving their lives for those they love, confronting evil and injustice, being healers and reconcilers in the world.

Why the cross? Because in contemplating the love of God revealed in the death and resurrection of Jesus and in trusting in the way of Jesus as a way to life, Christians under duress can persevere in their journey to God.

Why the cross? Because the community formed in the name of Jesus Crucified and Risen is a community that strives for mutual love and respect, is patient with weakness, is willing to forgive and be forgiven, a community that is, in fact, the body of the Crucified Christ who is triumphant but still bears the wounds of his cross, a community able to give a witness of hope and meaning to the world.

On the eve of his crucifixion, Jesus gathered his disciples for a final Passover meal. During the course of this Jewish festival celebrating Israel's deliverance from slavery and death, Jesus offers a final interpretation of what he faced. Taking bread, he broke it and said, "This is my body broken for you." Taking the cup of wine, he said, "This is my blood poured out for you for the forgiveness of sins." His death was an act of love, a giving of life that would endure in the face of evil and injustice, a revelation of God's redemptive love for the world.

He instructs his disciples: "Do this in memory of me." Live as I live; be sent as I am sent; love as I have loved you. This is the ultimate meaning of the cross of Christ.

O sacrum convivium!
in quo Christus sumitur:
recolitur memoria passionis eius:
mens impletur gratia:
et futurae gloriae nobis pignus datur.
Alleluia.
O sacred banquet!
in which Christ is received,
the memory of his Passion is renewed,
the mind is filled with grace,
and a pledge of future glory to us is given.
Alleluia.

—"*O Sacrum Convivium*," a Latin hymn composed by
Thomas Aquinas in 1264 and traditionally sung
on the feast of *Corpus Christi* ("the body of Christ")

Bibliography

Achtemeier, Paul. *1 Peter*. Hermeneia. Minneapolis: Fortress, 1998.

Allison, Dale C., Jr. *Constructing Jesus: Memory, Imagination, and History*. Grand Rapids: Baker, 2010.

Aristeas. *Letter of Aristeas to Philocrates*. The translation of the Letter is from that of R. J. H. Shutt in *The Old Testament Pseudepigrapha*. Edited by James H. Charlesworth. Vol. 2. Garden City, NY: Doubleday, 1985, 7–34.

Attridge, Harold W. *Hebrews*. Hermeneia. Philadelphia: Fortress, 1989.

Baker, Mark D., and Joel B. Green. *Recovering the Scandal of the Cross: Atonement in New Testament and Contemporary Contexts*. 2nd ed. Downers Grove, IL: InterVarsity, 2011.

Balch, David L., and Carolyn Osiek, eds. *Early Christian Families in Context: An Interdisciplinary Dialogue*. Grand Rapids: Eerdmans, 2003.

Barth, Markus. *Ephesians 1–3*. Anchor Bible 34. Garden City, NY: Doubleday, 1974.

Best, Ernest. *Ephesians*. ICC. Edinburgh: T & T Clark, 1998.

Bieringer, Rerimund, Didier Pollefeyt, and Frederique Vandecastelle-Vanneuville, eds. *Anti-Judaism and the Fourth Gospel*. Assen, the Netherlands: Royal Van Gorcum, 2001.

Brown, Raymond. *The Death of the Messiah: From Gethsemane to the Grave: A Commentary on the Passion Narratives in the Four Gospels*. 2 vols. New York: Doubleday, 1993.

———. *The Gospel according to John I–XII*. Garden City, NY: Doubleday, 1966.

———. *The Gospel according to John XIII–XXI*. Garden City, NY: Doubleday, 1970.

Brown, Schuyler. *Apostasy and Perseverance in the Theology of Luke*. Analecta Biblica 36. Rome: Pontifical Biblical Institute, 1969.

139

———. "The Costly Loss of Lament." *JSOT* 36 (1986): 57–71.

Brueggemann, Walter. *The Message of the Psalms*. Minneapolis: Augsburg, 1984.

Carroll, John T., and Joel B. Green. *The Death of Jesus in Early Christianity*. Peabody, MA: Hendrickson, 1995.

Carter, Warren. *The Roman Empire and the New Testament: An Essential Guide*. Nashville: Abingdon, 2006.

Chapman, David W. *Ancient Jewish and Christian Perceptions of Crucifixion*. Grand Rapids: Baker Academic, 2010.

Cicero. *Pro Rabirio Perduellionis Reo*. See *Cicero: Pro Lege Manilla, Pro Caecina, Pro Cluentio, Pro Rabirio Perduellionis*. With an English translation by H. Grose Hodge. Loeb Classical Library. London: Heinemann, 1927.

Collins, Adela Yarbro. *Mark*. Hermeneia. Minneapolis: Augsburg Fortress, 2007.

Cook, John Granger. "Crucifixion and Burial." *NTS* 57, no. 2 (April 2011): 193–213.

———. *Crucifixion in the Mediterranean World*. WUNT 327. Tubingen, Germany: Mohr Siebeck, 2014.

Cousar, Charles B. *A Theology of the Cross: The Death of Jesus in the Pauline Letters*. Overtures to Biblical Theology. Minneapolis: Fortress, 1990.

Cullmann, Oscar. "Immortality of the Soul or Resurrection of the Dead?" In *Immortality and Resurrection*, edited by K. Stendahl. New York: MacMillan, 1965.

Cuvillier, Elian. "La construction narrative de la mission dans le premier évangile; Un déplacement théologique et identitaire." In *The Gospel of Matthew at the Crossroads of Early Christianity*, edited by Donald Senior. BETL 243. Leuven, Belgium: Peeters, 2011.

Danker, Frederick W. "The Demonic Secret in Mark: A Reexamination of the Cry of Dereliction (15:34)." *ZNW* 61, nos. 1–2 (January 1970): 48–69.

———, ed. *A Greek-English Lexicon of the New Testament and Other Early Christian Literature*. 3rd ed. Chicago: University of Chicago Press, 2000.

Davies, W. D., and Dale C. Allison, Jr. *Matthew III, 19–28*. ICC. Edinburgh: T & T Clark, 1996.

De Boer, Martinus C. "Cross and Cosmos in Galatians." In *The Unrelenting God: God's Action in Scripture*, edited by David J. Downs and Matthew L. Skinner. Grand Rapids: Eerdmans, 2013.

De La Potterie, Ignace. *The Hour of Jesus: The Passion and the Resurrection of Jesus according to John*. New York: Alba House, 1989.

Dodd, C. H. *The Interpretation of the Fourth Gospel*. New York: Cambridge University Press, 1953.

Donahue, John R. *Are You the Christ?* SBL Dissertation Series 10. Missoula, MT: Scholars Press, 1973.

Donahue, John R., and Daniel J. Harrington. *The Gospel of Mark*. Sacra Pagina 2. Collegeville, MN: Liturgical Press, 2002.

Duke, Paul. *Irony in the Fourth Gospel*. Atlanta: John Knox Press, 1985.

Dunn, James D. G. *The Epistles to the Colossians and to Philemon*. NIGTC. Grand Rapids: Eerdmans, 1996.

———. *The Theology of Paul the Apostle*. Grand Rapids: Eerdmans, 1998.

Eberhart, Christen A. *The Sacrifice of Jesus: Understanding Atonement Biblically*. Minneapolis: Fortress, 2011.

Eiesland, Nancy L. *The Disabled God: Toward a Liberatory Theology of Disability*. Nashville: Abingdon, 1994.

Elliott, John H. *1 Peter*. Anchor Bible 37B. New York: Doubleday, 2000.

———. *A Home for the Homeless: A Sociological Exegesis of 1 Peter, Its Situation and Strategy*. Philadelphia: Fortress, 1981.

Elliott, Neil. "The Anti-Imperial Message of the Cross." In *Paul and Empire: Religion and Power in Roman Imperial Society*, edited by Richard Horsley. Harrisburg, PA: Trinity Press International, 1997.

Farelly, Nicolas. *The Disciples in the Fourth Gospel: A Narrative Analysis of Their Faith and Understanding*. WUNT 2/290. Tubingen, Germany: Mohr Siebeck, 2010.

Fehribach, Adeline. *The Women in the Life of the Bridegroom: A Feminist Historical-Literary Analysis of the Female Characters in the Fourth Gospel*. Collegeville, MN: Liturgical Press, 1998.

Finlan, Stephen. *Problems with Atonement*. Collegeville, MN: Liturgical Press, 2005.

Finney, Mark T. *Honour and Conflict in the Ancient World: 1 Corinthians in Its Greco-Roman Social Setting*. London: T & T Clark, 2012.

Fitzmyer, Joseph A. "Crucifixion in Ancient Palestine, Qumran Literature, and the New Testament." *CBQ* 40 (1978): 493–513.

141

————. *The Gospel according to Luke I–IX*. Anchor Bible 28. Garden City, NY: Doubleday, 1981.

Forestell, J. Terence. *The Word of the Cross*. Analecta Biblica 57. Rome: Biblical Institute Press, 1974.

Frederickson, David E. *Eros and the Christ: Longing and Envy in Paul's Christology*. Minneapolis: Fortress, 2013.

Garrett, Susan R. *The Demise of the Devil: Magic and the Demonic in Luke's Writings*. Minneapolis: Augsburg Fortress, 1989.

Gorman, Michael J. *Apostle of the Crucified Lord: A Theological Introduction to Paul & His Letters*. Grand Rapids: Eerdmans, 2004.

Green, Joel B. *The Death of Jesus*. WUNT 2/33. Tübingen, Germany: Mohr Siebeck, 1988.

————. "'He Saved Others; Let Him Save Himself': The Death of Jesus in the Gospel According to Luke." In John T. Carroll and Joel B. Green, *The Death of Jesus in Early Christianity*. Peabody, MA: Hendrickson, 1995.

————. "'Was It Not Necessary for the Messiah to Suffer These Things and Enter into His Glory?': The Significance of Jesus' Death for Luke's Soteriology." In *The Spirit and Christ in the New Testament and Christian Theology: Essays in Honor of Max Turner*, edited by Howard Marshall, Volker Rabens, and Cornelis Bennema. Grand Rapids: Eerdmans, 2012.

Gutierrez, Gustavo. *On Job: God-Talk and the Suffering of the Innocent*. Maryknoll, NY: Orbis, 1987.

Hagner, Donald A. *Matthew 14–28*. Word Biblical Commentary 33b. Dallas: Word Books, 1995.

Harrington, Daniel J. *Why Do We Suffer? A Scriptural Approach to the Human Condition*. Franklin, WI: Sheed and Ward, 2000.

Hays, Richard B. "Faithful Witness, Alpha and Omega: The Identity of Jesus in the Apocalypse of John." In *Revelation and the Politics of Apocalyptic Interpretation*, edited by Richard B. Hays and Stefan Alkier. Waco, TX: Baylor University Press, 2012.

Hengel, Martin. *The Atonement: The Origins of the Doctrine in the New Testament*. Philadelphia: Fortress, 1981.

————. *Crucifixion in the Ancient World and the Folly of the Message of the Cross*. Philadelphia: Fortress, 1977.

Horace. *Satires, Epistles and Ars Poetica*. Translated by H. Rushton Fairclough. Loeb Classical Library, no. 194. Cambridge, MA: Harvard University Press, 1926.

Horrell, David G., Bradley Arnold, and Travis B. Williams. "Visuality, Vivid Description, and the Message of 1 Peter: The Significance of the Roaring Lion (1 Peter 5:8)." *JBL* 132, no. 3 (2013): 697–716.

Hurtado, Larry W. *The Earliest Christian Artifacts: Manuscripts and Christian Origins.* Grand Rapids: Eerdmans, 2006.

———. "The Staurogram: Earliest Depiction of Jesus' Crucifixion." *Biblical Archaeology Review* 39, no. 2 (March–April 2013).

Irvine, Christopher. *The Cross and Creation in Christian Liturgy and Art.* London: SPCK, 2013.

Johnson, Luke Timothy. *Prophetic Jesus, Prophetic Church: The Challenge of Luke–Acts to Contemporary Christians.* Grand Rapids: Eerdmans, 2011.

Josephus. *Wars of the Jews.* See translation by William Whiston. *The Works of Josephus. Complete and Unabridged.* Peabody, MA: Hendrickson, 1987.

Juel, Donald. *Messiah and Temple.* SBL Dissertation Series 31. Missoula, MT: Scholars Press, 1977.

Karris, Robert J. *Luke: Artist and Theologian.* New York: Paulist Press, 1985.

Koester, Craig R. *Symbolism in the Fourth Gospel: Meaning, Mystery, Community.* 2nd ed. Minneapolis: Fortress, 2003.

———. "Why Was the Messiah Crucified? A Study of God, Jesus, Satan, and Human Agency in Johannine Theology." In *The Death of Jesus in the Fourth Gospel,* edited by G. Van Belle. BETL 200. Leuven, Belgium: Peeters, 2007.

Konradt, Matthias. *Israel, Kirche und die Völker im Matthäusevangelium.* WUNT 1/215. Tübingen, Germany: Mohr Siebeck, 2007.

Kraybill, J. Nelson. *Apocalypse and Allegiance: Worship, Politics, and Devotion in the Book of Revelation.* Grand Rapids: Brazos, 2010.

Kuhn, Heinz Wolfgang. "Die Kreuzesstrafe während der frühen Kaiserzeit: Ihre Wirklichkeit und Wertung in der Umwelt des Urchristentums." In *Augstieg und Niedergang der Römischen Welt,* edited by Wolfgang Haase. Vol. II.25.1. Berlin/New York: Walter de Gruyter, 1982.

Lee, Jae Won. "Pilate and the Crucifixion of Jesus in Luke–Acts." In *Luke–Acts and Empire: Essays in Honor of Robert L. Brawley,* edited by David Rhoads, David Esterline, and Jae Won Lee. Eugene, OR: Pickwick Publications, 2011.

MacDonald, Margaret Y. *Colossians, Ephesians.* Sacra Pagina 17. Collegeville, MN: Liturgical Press, 2000.

Matera, Frank J. *The Kingship of Jesus.* SBL Dissertation Series 66. Chico, CA: SBL Press, 1982.

———. *Passion Narratives and Gospel Theologies: Interpreting the Synoptics through Their Passion Stories*. New York: Paulist, 1986.

McCruden, Kevin B. "The Eloquent Blood of Jesus: The Neglected Theme of the Fidelity of Jesus in Hebrews 12:24." *CBQ* 75 (2013): 504–20.

McKnight, Scot. *A Community Called Atonement*. Nashville: Abingdon, 2007.

Meier, John P. *A Marginal Jew: Rethinking the Historical Jesus*. Vol. 3, *Companions and Competitors*. New York: Doubleday, 2001.

———. *A Marginal Jew: Rethinking the Historical Jesus*. Vol. 4, *Law and Love*. New Haven, CT: Yale University Press, 2009.

Mitchell, Alan C. *Hebrews*. Sacra Pagina 13. Collegeville, MN: Liturgical Press, 2007.

Moloney, Francis J. "Constructing Jesus and the Son of Man." *CBQ* 75 (2013): 719–38.

———. *The Gospel of John*. Sacra Pagina 4. Collegeville, MN: Liturgical Press, 1998.

———. *Love in the Gospel of John: An Exegetical, Theological, and Literary Study*. Grand Rapids: Baker Academic, 2013.

Moltmann, Jürgen. "The Cross as Military Symbol for Sacrifice." In *Cross Examinations: Readings on the Meaning of the Cross Today*, edited by Marit Trelstad. Minneapolis: Augsburg Fortress, 2006.

Morgan-Wynne, John. *The Cross in the Johannine Writings*. Eugene, OR: Pickwick, 2011.

Mounce, Robert H. *The Book of Revelation*. The New International Commentary on the New Testament. Grand Rapids: Eerdmans, 1998.

Perkins, Pheme. *Ephesians*. Abingdon New Testament Commentaries. Nashville: Abingdon, 1997.

Pesher Nahum. Cave 4; 11QTemple 64:6-13.

Plautus, Titus Maccius. *The Miles gloriosus of T. Maccius Plautus*. Edited by Robert Yelverton Tyrrell. London: Macmillan, 1881.

Porter, Stanley E. "Can Traditional Exegesis Enlighten Literary Analysis of the Fourth Gospel? An Examination of the Old Testament Fulfillment Motif and the Passover Theme." In *The Gospels and the Scriptures of Israel*, edited by Craig A. Evans and W. Richard Stegner. JSNTSup 104. Sheffield, UK: Sheffield Academic Press, 1994.

Quintillian. *The Lesser Declamations*. Vol. 1. Edited and translated by

D. R. Schackleton Bailey. Loeb Classical Library 500. Cambridge, MA: Harvard University Press, 2006.

Reid, Barbara. *Taking Up the Cross: New Testament Interpretations through Latina and Feminist Eyes.* Minneapolis: Augsburg Fortress, 2007.

Rindge, Matthew S. "Reconfiguring the Akedah and Recasting God: Lament and Divine Abandonment in Mark." *JBL* 131, no. 4 (2012): 755–74.

Roetzel, Calvin J. *The Letters of Paul: Conversations in Context.* 4th ed. Louisville: Westminster John Knox, 1998.

Rowe, C. Kavin. *World Upside Down: Reading Acts in the Graeco-Roman Age.* New York: Oxford University Press, 2009.

Rubenstein, Richard. *My Brother Paul.* New York: Harper and Row, 1972.

Ryan, Robin. *God and the Mystery of Human Suffering: A Theological Conversation across the Ages.* New York: Paulist, 2011.

Samuelsson, Gunnar. *Crucifixion in Antiquity: An Inquiry into the Background and Significance of the New Testament Terminology of Crucifixion.* Tübingen, Germany: Mohr Siebeck, 2011.

Sanders, E. P. *Paul and Palestinian Judaism: A Comparison of Patterns of Religion.* Philadelphia: Fortress, 1977.

Schnelle, Udo. *Apostle Paul: His Life and Theology.* Grand Rapids: Baker Academic, 2005.

Schüssler Fiorenza, Elizabeth. *Revelation: Vision of a Just World.* Proclamation Commentaries. Minneapolis: Fortress, 1981.

Seneca, Epistle 101 to Lucilius. See *Moral Letters to Lucilius.* Translated by Robert Mott Gummere. Loeb Classical Library. Vol. 3. Cambridge, MA: Harvard University Press, 1925.

Senior, Donald. "The Death of Jesus and the Resurrection of the Holy Ones, Matthew 27:51–53." *CBQ* 38 (1976): 312–29.

————. "The Death of Jesus as Sign: A Fundamental Johannine Ethic." In *The Death of Jesus in the Fourth Gospel,* edited by G. Van Belle. BETL 200. Leuven, Belgium: Peeters, 2007.

————, ed. *The Gospel of Matthew at the Crossroads of Early Christianity.* BETL 243. Leuven, Belgium: Peeters, 2011.

————. "Matthew at the Crossroads of Early Christianity: An Introductory Assessment." In *The Gospel of Matthew at the Crossroads of Early Christianity,* edited by D. Senior. BETL 243. Leuven, Belgium: Peeters, 2011.

145

———. *The Passion Narrative according to Matthew: A Redactional Study.* BETL 39. Leuven, Belgium: Leuven University Press, 1975.

———. *The Passion of Jesus in the Gospel of John.* The Passion Series 4. Collegeville, MN: Liturgical Press, 1991.

———. *The Passion of Jesus in the Gospel of Luke.* The Passion Series 3. Collegeville, MN: Liturgical Press, 1989.

———. *The Passion of Jesus in the Gospel of Mark.* The Passion Series 2. Collegeville, MN: Liturgical Press, 1984.

———. *The Passion of Jesus in the Gospel of Matthew.* The Passion Series 1. Collegeville, MN: Liturgical Press, 1985.

Senior, Donald, and Daniel J. Harrington, *1 Peter, Jude and 2 Peter.* Sacra Pagina 15. Collegeville, MN: Liturgical Press, 2003.

Simundson, Daniel J. *Faith under Fire: Biblical Interpretations of Suffering.* Minneapolis: Augsburg, 1980.

Stendahl, Krister. *Paul among Jews and Gentiles.* Philadelphia: Fortress, 1976.

Tambasco, Anthony J. *The Bible on Suffering: Social and Political Implications.* New York: Paulist, 2001.

Thielman, Frank. *From Plight to Solution: A Jewish Framework for Understanding Paul's View of the Law in Galatians and Romans.* NovTSup. Eugene, OR: Wipf and Stock, 1989.

Thompson, Leonard L. *Revelation.* Abingdon New Testament Commentaries. Nashville: Abingdon, 1998.

Thurston, Bonnie. *Philippians & Philemon.* Sacra Pagina 10. Collegeville, MN: Liturgical Press, 2005.

Travis, Stephen H. *Christ and the Judgment of God: The Limits of Divine Retribution in New Testament Thought.* Peabody, MA: Hendrickson, 2008.

Trelstad, Marit, ed. *Cross Examinations: Readings on the Meaning of the Cross Today.* Minneapolis: Augsburg Fortress, 2006.

Van Belle, G., ed. *The Death of Jesus in the Fourth Gospel.* BETL 200. Leuven, Belgium: Peeters, 2007.

Vearncombe, Erin. "Cloaks, Conflict, and Mark 14:51-52." *CBQ* 75 (2013): 683–703.

Waltke, Bruce K., James M. Houston, and Erika Moore. *The Psalms as Christian Lament: A Historical Commentary.* Grand Rapids: Eerdmans, 2014.

146

Whitaker, Robyn. "Rebuke or Recall? Rethinking the Role of Peter in Mark's Gospel." *CBQ* 75 (2013): 666–82.

Wilson, R. McL. *Colossians and Philemon*. ICC. London: T & T Clark, 2005.

Wright, N. T. *Paul and the Faithfulness of God*. 2 vols. Minneapolis: Fortress, 2013.

———. "Revelation and Christian Hope: Political Implications of the Revelation to John." In *Revelation and the Politics of Apocalyptic Interpretation*, edited by Richard B. Hays and Stefan Alkier. Waco, TX: Baylor University Press, 2012.

Zias, Joseph, and Eliezer Sekeles. "The Crucified Man from Giv'at ha-Mivtar: A Reappraisal." *IEJ* 35, no. 1 (1985): 22–27.

Index of Scriptures

149

John

Apocrypha

Wisdom of Solomon

Sirach

Baruch

Index of Modern Authors

161

Index of Subjects

165

CPSIA information can be obtained at www.ICGtesting.com
Printed in the USA
LVOW06s0053011014

406589LV00007B/13/P